What Others are Saying about *Women Riders Who Could... and Did*

"There are many successful equestriennes ... Yet it seems the media loves the horseman. Karma Kitaj's book brings the light back to the female side of this world, giving women readers the role models that previously lived in the shadows. They show us the trail to success."

—**Donna Snyder-Smith**, *Coach of Equestrian Biomechanics/Author of* The Complete Guide to Endurance Riding and Competition *and 2 other books, Lifetime Achievement Award from the American Riding Instructors Association, AHSA Judge*

"It's inspiring to read about the lives of so many successful horsewomen—their accomplishments, their individuality and the simple things that make them seem like one of us. It's the latter that makes us think that if they can do it, maybe we can! And it's their unique strength and determination in the face of adversity that sets them apart and gives us something to strive for."

— **Julie Goodnight** *of Goodnight Training, Inc.*

"Women have a harder time in the horse world ... If a woman is successful, you can be sure she deserves it. The women Karma Kitaj writes about deserve our attention and admiration ... It's a worthwhile book for young riders who aspire to be professionals. The stories of these women will give them the courage to try for the best even though they have encountered challenges."

—**Cindy Sydnor**, *Long-listed for the U.S. Olympic Team, Dressage Instructor, "R" dressage judge, USDF Examiner for Certification Program*

Women Riders
Who Could . . . And Did

Women Riders Who Could ... And Did

Life Stories of Top Level Equestriennes

by KARMA KITAJ

Foreword by Sharon McKusker,
FEI Dressage trainer, USDF Gold Medalist.

Women Riders Who Could ... And Did: Life Stories of Top Level Equestriennes

By Karma Kitaj
Published by Huckle Hill Press
www.HuckleHillPress.com
P.O. Box 67273
Chestnut Hill, Massachusetts 02467

Publisher's Cataloging in Publication

Kitaj, Karma.
Women riders who could ... and did: life stories of
top level equestriennes / by Karma Kitaj.
p. cm.
Includes bibliographical references and index.
LCCN 2009907634
ISBN-13: 978-0-9715957-3-6
ISBN-10: 0-9715957-3-9
1. Women in horse sports—Biography.
2. Women in horse sports—Interviews. I. Title.
SF284.5.K58 2009 798.2'092'2
QBI09-600157

Permission granted for use:
p. xii: From *Gawani Pony Boy, Of Women and Horses*
(Irvine, CA: BowTiePress).
Reprinted with permission of BowTiePress.

pp. 49, 51, 52, 56: From *Riding For My Life* by Julie Krone.
Copyright © 1995 by Julie Krone.
By permission of Little, Brown & Company.

pp. 142, 143, 144: From *Centered Riding 2: Further Exploration* by Sally Swift.
By permission of publisher, Trafalgar Square Books, N. Pomfret, VT.

Photography credits, see pp. 200

Book design by Cathleen Shaw at www.ShawCreativeGroup.com

Printed in the United States of America
Provided by Quality Books, Inc.

Dedication

To my husband Jeff Cooper, who has been my unwavering booster and companion in horsemanship; he started riding in middle age, because I wanted to do so. He supported this book in every way – by facilitating some of my journeys to interview women from Colorado to Texas to Hawaii, by reading and critiquing the manuscript, by encouraging me to finish it after a long lapse, and by marketing it to horsey friends. Not to mention the computer emergencies he responded to along the way. Without him, this book wouldn't have been what it is.

Acknowledgements

So many people contribute to a book, in ways known and unknown to me as the author; it's not only that they've contributed to the book's making, but to me as an equestrienne. These people have informed me as a rider and taught me to keep pushing through obstacles in my body and mind. They've added to my ease in constructing this book and turning my love of horses into something more permanent. Here are the people who come to mind.

Thank you to Lise Beane, a creative public relations person whom I met through networking in Boston years ago. She had read my first book and asked what I'd do next. I had no idea, but she offered: "Why not write about lives of famous horsewomen?" That idea appealed to me, a newly passionate horse person myself and I ran with it. I'm grateful for her sharing her intuition with me.

Then my riding instructors – finally, I had found good ones. I had written about my "*Discovering Horses at Age 50*," (http://www.lifespring-coaching.com/articles.htm). It had not been easy for me to find intuitive, well trained, and ethical coaches who were also good at teaching their skill. Jaana Sheehan, who first taught me dressage and later found me my present horse, Diamond, was one of the first people like that.

Later, I joined my husband in taking weekly lessons from eventer Jess Systo. I had thought she taught more advanced riders, but she titrated her instruction so that it would be just right for me and my horse to learn correct flatwork. She's had the guts to push me, not let me get away with succumbing to my fears of riding in the ½ seat at the canter or even jumping over a low fence, always encouraging me with "I know you can do it." Now, my horse has even learned to ride with energy from behind, not a simple feat for this 17 year old Morgan, who was out of control when I got him.

Next, our friend Ted Gewanter, Western rider and inveterate reader of all things equestrian, gave me ideas about famous women to interview and to ask for endorsements for the book. He was always willing to offer advice and encouragement, despite his critical nature. I trust his praise, as he's thoroughly honest when he doesn't agree with something I write or say.

Susanna Sturgis, my editor, patiently reconstructed all of the manuscript to make it more compelling and to make each chapter flow better. An equestrienne herself, she knew enough (or took the trouble to Google for the information) to ask tough questions when something I wrote didn't make sense to her or when some piece of information was missing. I ended up having to go back to most of the women to clarify or update, as Susanna wouldn't let me get away with anything less than an exemplary product.

A note of thanks to people on the listserv www.selfpublishing@yahoogroups.com for always being there to help me find just the right people to help me put this project together. They helped me to find Susanna and also Kay Dusheck, another equestrienne, who did a professional job of creating an index.

Next, Cathleen Shaw of www.ShawCreativeGroup.com, a beautiful book designer, did the cover and interior design. With tremendous patience, she kept changing that front cover so that the woman on horseback had as nearly as possible the appropriate form while sitting on her horse. She also chose fonts and sensitively embedded the photographs in each chapter. It turned out to be just what I wanted.

I appreciate Sharon McKusker's willingness to write a foreword, especially as she knows me only through her student, my former instructor, Jaana Sheehan. I also am thrilled that so many excellent horsewomen agreed to write testimonials and are excited about the book – they remind me why a book about women in high-level sports is important; yes, sexism still abounds.

I am grateful to the professional photographers who gave complimentary photos to be included in each of the chapters – realizing that this book was created as a hobby, not as my vocation, they were willing to merely get credit and a book upon completion. I regret that despite our persistent efforts, there are still a couple of photos, taken decades ago, where we have not been able to identify the photographers to give them appropriate credit.

Finally, I can never express my gratitude enough for the women whom I interviewed, who probably didn't know what they were getting into. Each one responded with patience and enthusiasm to my persistent requests for yet one more follow up question. Most ended up giving me hours of their time, either while hosting me at their ranches and barns or, subsequently, on phone or email interviews. Their life stories, precious to me, have given me inspiration to keep pushing in areas that are hard for me, whether in the sport of riding or in life itself. They have added to my list of role models, truly the 'women who could and did."

Contents

Foreword

I've been a horsey person forever. My family moved from the New York suburbs to the New Hampshire countryside when I was ten. I had had some exposure to horses during summer vacations as a young girl, but once settled into our NH farm, my life changed forever. My parents bought me my first horse at a local "hack" auction and I was hooked. I rode everything – quarter horses, morgans, welsh ponies, draft crosses, appaloosas, paints, thoroughbreds and Warmbloods. I tried all the disciplines from Western, to hunt seat, saddle seat, 3-day eventing and, finally, dressage. Horses were my world as a girl and my father thought for sure I would grow out of it. Recently at age 90, my dad attended the US National Grand Prix Dressage Championships where I competed and finished **seventh in the country!** It goes to show that there are some things you just never grow out of. And, at 47, I expect to be involved with horses for decades more.

My accomplished dressage student Jaana Sheehan popped the question to me last year: How would you like to write a foreword for a friend's book about famous equestriennes? Karma Kitaj – you'd never guess she's in her sixties — recently started taking lessons with Jaana. She'd been bucked up seven feet in the air and broke her hip and after six weeks on crutches, she was back "in the saddle," but looking for a new horse that was bombproof. "I happened to find a little Lippitt Morgan gelding for her – she loved him at first sight," Jaana told me, "but neither of us had any idea he'd be such a challenge. She just stuck with him until he settled down and he became a love."

Karma's experience as a mature woman who had not grown up with horses intrigued me as someone who'd been immersed in the horse world since I was a kid. How did she come to be so passionate about horsemanship that she takes lessons every week all year long? And in New England, no less. And she was so curious about horses that she decided to travel all over the country on her own dime, interviewing famous equestriennes in their barns and ranches and then writing and publishing a book about it. I decided I had to accept the invitation to read the book and write a for word.

And what makes me qualified to introduce such a book? I am fortunate to be able to make a living doing what I love – training and working with horses – not many people do that. As a professional trainer it's always fascinated me to learn about how other horse women got their start. My work has taken me all over the country and the world – competing, looking for horses, and riding with top dressage trainers. I've competed in many of the top US dressage competitions and have been fortunate to train with several top trainers – Klaus Balkenhol, Michael Poulin, Pamela Goodrich, and Carol Lavell, to name a few. One of the things this sport teaches you is that you never stop learning. Every horse is a new opportunity for knowledge. As demonstrated in this book, the sport allows for longevity, so many riders are competitive well past their 40's. And, imagine how long people can ride recreationally – into their eighties, for certain.

Women Riders Who Could – And Did not only outlines how these ladies made it to the top of their individual niches within the horse world, but it gives the reader insight into the passion that carries them through their careers. Passion is something I always felt that horse people share – for these women the obstacles they had to overcome and the commitment they had to their dream of working with horses is inspiring.

Karma Kitaj also details the journey that these equestriennes took as they honed their skills and developed into the world-class horsewomen they are today. Each rider, aged forty and up into their nineties when Karma talked to them, developed from their experiences a unique niche which they ultimately excelled in. They all learned from their tough times and grew as a result of them. They made their weaknesses into their strengths and found ways to lead passionate, fulfilled lives through their work with horses. The book is an enjoyable and compelling read for the aspiring adult newcomer to horses as well as the woman who was a dedicated Pony Clubber in her youth. It leaves you feeling full of the hope and inspiration that comes from working with these wonderful animals.

— **Sharon McKusker**

FEI Dressage trainer

USET Long listed dressage rider

USDF Gold Medalist

Souhegan Farm

Ashby, MA

Introduction

"In our dreams we charge over hedges on a perfect frosty morning at the hunt. We race down the last furlong in the come-from-behind win of the year. We stun judges in a sequined satin jacket atop a glossy plump champion pleasure horse. We ride on the beach with abandon at sunset ... We are the horse — that sweet, grassy breathing; the salty, earthy smell; the soft, inquisitive gaze, the wild, courageous heart; the light, powerful stride; the silky, flying mane."

—From Lisa Kiser, in *Gawani Pony Boy, Of Women and Horses*

I was not one of those nine-year-old girls who read *The Black Stallion* series many times over, collected Breyer horse figurines, and pestered my parents for a horse of my very own. I never saw a horse in my childhood, except at Catskill Game Farm, where I offered treats to ponies, along with baby llamas and baby goats. I never even watched TV Westerns. Even though I grew up in Troy, a small city in upper New York State, one that was 15-minutes' drive to horse country, my mother would have been too nervous to allow any of her children to ride horses.

No, I didn't discover horses until I was an adult. I had a fantasy of "riding off into the sunset," my then-long brown hair flying in the breeze (no helmet in those days!). My husband gave me 10 riding lessons for my 40th birthday at Dana Hall School in Wellesley, Massachusetts, a few towns away from where we live. Ten lessons! I thought that would surely give me the skills I needed to ride. Little did I know that twenty-five years later, having owned five different horses in the last dozen years, I'm still taking a lesson every week. There's no end to learning on a horse.

Having grown up in the nineteen-fifties, way before Title IX mandated equal opportunities in schools, I was not exposed to sports much. I was the kid who slipped to the back of the line in gym so I wouldn't have to go up to bat. No one had ever taught me how to hold the bat, much less to keep my eyes on the ball to contact it. Besides, I didn't like to sweat so I avoided physical activity. Horses have given me a chance to connect with my body, an opportunity that younger women had more experience with, because sports were readily available and encouraged for girls.

After my husband and I moved to rural Massachusetts for weekends, we discovered it was horse country. What better way to express my dream fantasy of riding off into the sunset! I bought my first horse, a three-year-old Quarter Horse mare named Esther Gold Star; we called her "Etoile," French for "star." I had bought Etoile sight unseen upon my instructor's recommendation. She wasn't a good horse for me, a new middle-aged, timid rider — she was too young, too marish, too stubborn. But, despite the challenges of riding her, I quickly fell in love with her and wanted to ride as much as possible.

What was it that attracted me to horses as an adult? Surely, the majestic quality of their bodies, the athletic movements, the smell of their hay-sweet breath, the feeling of a 1,000-pound animal moving beneath me, the thrill of being able to control a powerful creature by using the most subtle seat and leg and arm movements — all these experiences are part of the picture. Women and girls are notoriously smitten with horses' strength, power, and beauty; more so than men, females seem to develop an emotional bond with horses.

But, loving horses for me was more than just my admiration for them. By nature I'm a lover of learning. I live more in my "head" than in my body. I have been someone who strives and plans and ponders. I love reading and writing. I discovered that these qualities are of minimal use when it comes to riding a horse.

What I've come to appreciate about being with horses is the opportunity to connect with the present moment and to be *in* my body. This was a new experience for me. I'd done well in school and had a satisfying career, first as a psychotherapist and more recently as a life coach, but I'd never been so totally involved and engaged, so "in the moment," as I was on horseback. Being around horses is a joyful experience and a compelling one. I never refuse to go to the barn to ride, even in nasty weather or in the darkness and frigid temperatures of a New England winter evening, after working all day and traveling two hours to our country house.

What appeals to me so much about horses? I love watching my Morgan gelding, Diamond, playing with his buddies in the pasture, rearing up on their hind legs, nipping their pasture-mates, galloping along with their tails flying. Or bucking in glee on a particularly cool day after many hot ones. So free and unselfconscious. I love to observe their predictable horsey behavior — after I've carefully groomed Diamond's coat and returned him to his pasture, yup, he starts to scratch the surface of the ground and plops down on his favorite sandy spot for a good massage of his back, then ungracefully rises and shakes off only half of the dirt he's embedded in his once shiny coat. Then he, all 14.3 hands of him, makes his way to the shelter wherein lies all the hay he'd want, puts his ears back in a subtle gesture of command, and all the horses, much bigger than he, march right out, making room for His Majesty, the dominant one in his herd.

Horses are such exquisitely physically attuned creatures, they recognize the slightest muscle tension in their riders and discomfort in their handlers. So, it's forced me to notice what is in my body at any moment. Since my horse is especially sensitive, he's coached me to be equally observant of myself. If he is going too fast or jigging on the trail (his reaction to my stress), I scan my body for tension in my upper arms, shoulders, lower back, or legs that I might be transferring to him. As I'm experienced in doing this now, it has generalized to other moments, when I might be tense about giving a talk or being late or having a difficult conversation. Diamond has taught me how to recover within seconds and return to the present.

It was this awareness of being in the moment with horses that propelled me to explore what people call "spirituality." It gives me a day-to-day experience with letting go of worries about the past or the future. That learning has had ripple effects in the rest of my life. Despite the tumultuous times we live in, I can remain in the present and am seeking ways to complement my horsey life with other presencing activities, like meditation. Being present, as any experienced meditator or spiritual teacher will tell us, leads to a sense of peacefulness and at-oneness-with-the-world.

How did I move from recognizing what I get from horses to writing a book about women and horses? Some years ago, I was talking with Lise Beane, a creative PR person I met through networking channels in Boston. Since she knew about my first book, *Women Who Could — and Did*, which was based on stories of high-achieving scientists and artists, and my passion for the horse world, she said, "Why don't you write about famous horse women?" That was a no-brainer, but one I had to hear from someone else, because it hadn't occurred to me.

What would it have been like to have been involved with horses at a young age, to grow into adulthood with horses at the center of my life? The stories in this book of highly accomplished and successful horsewomen offer some answers to that question. What challenges did these women face, and how did they overcome them? The book became a collection of life stories and photographs that depict thirteen high-achieving horsewomen – often with their guard down, sometimes with tears in their eyes, reflecting on their passions, their learning, their regrets, and their joys. In the process of telling their life story, they describe the equestrian skill they know and love and give us an opportunity to learn the subtleties of disciplines such as endurance riding or Western cutting that we may know little about.

How would I decide which women and which disciplines to select? I used what's called a "snowball sample" in the research world, one where one thing led to another. As I engaged one woman to interview, she led me to others whom she admired or trained with. The women come from different disciplines, including dressage, show jumping, eventing, endurance, Western reining, cutting, barrel racing, trick riding, and race riding. Several equestrian disciplines are missing, such as polo, carriage driving, horse breeding, and hunt seat, but the women I interviewed often had experiences with other disciplines in their training.

One of the synchronicities of this project is that the women have learned from and pay tribute to one another: eventer Carol Kozlowski trained with show jumper Anne Kursiski and dressage coach Jane Savoie; centered riding master trainer Lucile Bump is a protégée of the late Sally Swift, but also trained with Linda Tellington-Jones. Race rider Julie Krone owes her success as a female in a male world to Kathy Kusner's efforts decades ago to be the first woman to get a license to race. And many of the women refer to each other as their role models.

What did I learn from these women, all modest about their <accomplishments, who had achieved more than they ever imagined they would? Just as I pushed my limits, physically and mentally, by discovering horses in middle age, the women I met also were distinguished by the extent to which they pushed their limits and reaped the benefit of doing so with stellar accomplishments. They went to the Olympics, they published books, they are Triple Crown winners, and they are sought after clinicians and coaches.

I was intrigued with the fact that so many of these women got to the top levels of their discipline through their own determination and perseverance. None of them were pampered and given expensive horses to compete with as youngsters. They made do, in many instances, with two-hundred dollar horses they paid for themselves as children by working at barns to pay for lessons; they often rode bareback because their families had no money for saddles.

These thirteen women shared from their hearts what it has been like for them to learn, practice, and excel in sports where women were not always welcomed and with minimal support from their families. Ages forty through ninety-plus when I met them, all of them were still engaged in equestrian activities. The women, regardless of their age, represent an ideal of positive, vital aging, something that I, at age sixty-five, hoping to ride for decades more, find inspirational. They challenged their own and others' expectations into their fifties, sixties, and beyond. What has been their formula for success and fulfillment?

Only four of these women grew up in families who had any knowledge of horses. Race rider Julie Krone's mother, a talented equestrienne herself, drove her to Churchill Downs in Kentucky from Eau Claire, Michigan on high school break to make sure she'd get a job at the track for the coming summer, initiating her race-riding life. Linda Tellington-Jones grew up in a family that rode and competed together for fun. As a child, she had lots of opportunity to become competent around horses and other farm animals as her father gave her responsibility for working on the family farm, just as he gave it to his sons. Anne Kursinski was introduced to the horse world via her mother, who was a recreational rider at a prestigious barn in California. She got the message from her mother, "You can do anything you want to do." Karen Womack Vold had to work to convince her rodeoing Dad that she was determined to trick ride. Once convinced, he became her booster.

The other women's parents tolerated their daughters' interest, worried about them, or ignored them. Olympic show jumper Kathy Kusner asserts that her parents never came to her competitions. Some remember their mothers being so afraid of horses that they wouldn't even hold a lead line with a horse at the other end. The majority of these top-level women had to be determined and independent about getting the experiences they so desired. Because of lack of funds or lack of interest from their families, some of those who rose to the top of their sport did so with little instruction and minimal tack. Valerie Kanavy won two world championships as a 100-mile endurance rider with not one lesson, since her family couldn't afford them when she was growing up. Former reining competitor Roberta McCarty rode, trained horses and riders and competed with no formal instruction.

What propelled these women to pursue a career with horses with so little backing and encouragement from their families as children? All of the women had an early, passionate attraction to horses or to animals in general. They were proactive in getting the information they needed through reading, intent observation of riders better than they, by immersing themselves in the world of the barn, and riding without equipment if that was the only choice. They devoted their out-of-school time as children to mucking out stalls in neighborhood barns to fund their lessons or pay for board for the horses they succeeded in purchasing for money they themselves often earned. As adolescents and young adults, they began to attract the attention of mentors because of their passion and perseverance.

They were willing to push their limits. Valerie Kanavy trailered her horse to college by herself, with no plan for where she was going to board him nor how she could afford to feed him. Jane Savoie continued riding after a horse accident injured her jaw, putting her out of commission and in pain for years. Karen Vold insisted upon trick riding, despite her beloved father's warnings about safety and the unsavory behaviors of cowboys in rodeo.

With some of the women, pushing their limits meant taking physical risks on a horse. Many of the women recall with amusement when as kids they rode bareback over rough terrain, racing their horses through the snow and ice, jumping onto their moving horses from the rear. Julie Krone was notorious for doing stunts on her horse — standing on his back while he galloped full-speed towards the barn door and dismounting just in time to avoid being decapitated. Other women pushed their limits in mental ways; Jane Savoie visioned herself competing in the Olympics, even though she was twenty-five pounds overweight, smoked, and had no money for a top-level horse.

As many girls and women report, some of them turned to their horses for comfort during a stressful period of their lives. Parents' divorce, abuse, alcoholism, rejection from peers, academic and physical challenges — all of these conditions receded as they visited the barn and started to groom their horses. Most of them were resilient in overcoming personal or cultural obstacles to attain the success they have achieved. None were given things they needed without a struggle. They all had fortitude, determination, and perseverance to get to where they are now.

Even those women who reported loving relationships with their parents had to be independent in pursuing their passion, as their families were not capable or knowledgeable about equestrian careers. They didn't get a ticket to success from their families. Each had to work hard, use their innate talents to be at the right place at the right time with the requisite skills to get what they wanted.

Most of the women have an intense curiosity that propels them to want to learn all they can about their sport, about taking the best care of their horses, about forming a relationship with the horses they encounter, and about how to effectively train others. Even though some elected not to go to college, they never stop learning. It's another way they challenge themselves and push their limits.

In meeting these lively, dedicated women, I've once again added to my list of role models, of "women who could — and did," women who have stretched themselves, physically and mentally, and continue to do so. My hope is that you, the reader, will also gain inspiration from their stories and never imagine that you don't have what it takes to do whatever you want.

—*Karma Kitaj*

Linda Tellington-Jones

Visionary Equine Ambassador

"I'm just getting started. I've never had more clarity, drive, health, or intent as I do now."

Internationally renowned as an animal trainer and healer, inventor, and author, Linda Tellington-Jones has won the hearts of animal lovers on five continents for her innovative and successful methods of enhancing health and happiness not only for horses but for humans, zoo animals, and companion animals as well. Her fifteen books have been translated into twelve languages; there are now more than 1,300 practitioners of the Tellington Method working in twenty-six countries. In 1992, the American Riding Instructors Association honored her with its Lifetime Achievement Award. In 1994, the North American Horsemen's Association named her Horsewoman of the Year.

The method that bears her name, TTEAM (Tellington TTouch Equine Awareness Method), is a system of body work (TTouch) and ground and riding exercises designed to enhance performance and health in horses. TTEAM combines Feldenkrais bodywork methods with ground and riding exercises that are designed to enhance the animal's confidence, coordination, and overall functioning. Linda has described TTouch as "like a language without words that allows us to communicate and understand our animal friends." She and her disciples around the world have trained riders and horses at all levels of experience and expertise, from the amateur rider or the green horse all the way up to those competing at the Olympic level.

Linda's Childhood in Rural Canada – She Excels in Horsemanship Early On

Not surprisingly, Linda, born Linda Hood, started her life as an animal lover and was encouraged by her parents, who taught her and her five younger siblings the value of human and animal life. She grew up on her family's large dairy and grain farm near Edmonton, Alberta, Canada. When she was six, her father gave her her first pony. Ginger became her constant companion. In those days, there were no school buses in that rural area. Walk the two and a half miles to school or ride horseback? What kind of choice was that? Linda rode bareback — no saddles were available — to her cousins' house and they would ride the rest of the way to school together. By age eight Linda was petitioning her parents for riding lessons. They agreed, if she would get a job in a barn to help pay for them.

Young though she was, Linda made her own arrangement at Briarcrest

Stables, a horse barn near the family's farm, which happened to be run by a well-regarded instructor, Alice Greaves Metheral. Despite the harsh weather of western Canada, Linda rode every day, rain or snow, from the time she was eight until she was fourteen. There were no indoor arenas in those days, but they did have lights in the outdoor ring, so she could ride into the evening. The stable had high-quality show horses, including Thoroughbreds, hunters, and Western pleasure horses. They also had a string of trail horses that people could rent on weekends. Linda's job included getting these horses ready for the renters and also helping to train and condition the show horses. Each day after school she'd exercise three or four young horses. She became known as a girl who could "stick on anything."

One evening a week, Alice Metheral gave a two-hour seminar on different aspects of horsemanship for the youngsters who worked for her; Linda learned at an early age about feeding, training, and judging different horse breeds.

During these years, she was also helping out on the family farm. She remembers driving a hayrake, a challenging job for a ten-year-old. Her father considered her just as valuable as the male farmhands and paid her for the hours she worked after school and in summers. She still remembers her grandfather taking her to the bank to open her first savings account, into which she deposited the money she was earning by raking hay and driving horses from sunup until sunset. Although she was the oldest child in the family, she did not have to do housework or child care because her mother always hired help, unusual for a farm family. So she could devote herself to working with the animals.

"I have amazing parents," Linda says now. "My dad died at ninety-three playing golf. No matter what we did, we knew that my parents loved us. Someone asked my dad which one of the kids he loved the most, and he said, without thinking, 'The one I'm with.' "When Linda's father died, he and her mother had been happily married for fifty-six years.

Everyone in the family was comfortable on horseback, but Linda was the one who took most strongly to equestrian activities. By age eleven, Linda was riding in major shows in western Canada. As a teenager she "catch rode," riding horses for other people. She won in every discipline she tried, including Western and English pleasure.

To teach a horse to jump, Mrs. Metheral would "get this long bullwhip and she'd chase the horse over the jump with me, the kid, riding." Mrs. Metheral used to let the horses "buck out" in the riding pen, a practice that bothered Linda, even as a child. After a horse was bucked out, its head would be tied to the saddle horn of the instructor's horse and Linda would get on. They would walk, trot, and canter like this until the horse stopped bucking and then the horse would be released from the other horse's saddle horn. Nobody wore a helmet in those days, and Linda got bucked off quite a bit. Although she hit her head a lot — she jokes that she's shorter than all her sisters because she fell on her head so often — she does not remember ever breaking anything. Although this method seems abusive to us now, Linda says it was common in those days.

Thanks to those early experiences, falling and bouncing became second nature. Not long ago, at the age of sixty-nine, Linda was training a client's horse, trotting along quietly, when with no warning the horse acted like it had been "hit by a cattle prod" and did a 180 degree turn. She was blown off and "felt like I was a 747, landing." She landed on her feet, without a bruise.

One day when Linda was twelve, an old man who lived nearby hobbled out with his cane and stopped her on her way home from the barn. He had been a cavalry officer in his younger days, circa 1880, and remained interested in horsemanship; he had watched her ride every day, he told her. He brought her a book about training young horses under saddle.

Rather than just slap a saddle on an unprepared horse, chase him around the round pen, and let him buck it out, the book showed how to ground-drive young horses first and then introduce the saddle gradually. Linda decided to test this method with one of the horses on the family farm, a sixteen-hand two-and-a-half-year-old Thoroughbred who had never been ridden. "So I took the book out to the barn and went through the steps with her," Linda says. "I remember the first time I mounted her and just rode her off. Totally understood what you wanted, because she knew how to turn and stop. Absolutely not afraid."

Her experience confirmed what her maternal grandfather, the horseman Will Caywood, practiced when he started a young horse. He would let a horse gradually become accustomed to his presence, humming, singing, or whistling to help it stay calm. She believes that these methods were at least partly responsible for her success in the show ring. "My attitude whenever I got on a horse I didn't know is to make the horse feel good," she says, "not to show him who's boss, but to say, 'how can we go in the show ring and have a really nice time'. So I won way more than my fair share, because it was an attitude that I had. Horses do understand when you acknowledge them and encourage them instead of trying to control or dominate them."

Calgary had huge shows that lasted as many as nine days. Linda showed in all categories. A typical equitation class might include between forty and sixty horses, with hunt seat and saddle seat riders competing against each other. The top contenders would be further tested by switching horses and then riding a pattern on horses they did not know. By the time Linda was fifteen she had retired the Calgary Herald Challenge Equitation trophy by winning it three times.

At one show, Linda told a judge from Toronto that she'd received an offer to ride professionally for a stable in Vancouver. The judge told her to get an education first and then decide what she wanted to do with her horsemanship. As it turned out, however, Linda's "education" didn't come through the conventional progression from secondary school to college. When she was only eighteen, she met and married her first husband, Wentworth Tellington, so she left both Canada and formal schooling behind. Much later she went to the University of California at Santa Cruz and UCLA night school and summer school.

Marriage to Went Tellington Was an Education of Many Sorts

Went Tellington was an American engineer who was then working in Canada. He was twenty years Linda's senior, a sophisticated Renaissance man whose knowledge and cultured tastes intrigued her. He had graduated from the military college at Norwich University, Vermont, in 1937, the year Linda was born; as a cavalry officer, he had competed at Madison Square Gardens. He later taught polo at West Point. He had a literary bent as well and introduced her both to classic literature and to creative writing. Always a good student, she learned to speed-read and read all of the classics, including *The Iliad* and *The Odyssey*, found in her husband's huge personal library. She started writing, thanks to Went's creative writing class. "I wouldn't be who I am, if not for Went," Linda says.

After a stint in Puerto Rico, where for the first time since she was six Linda did not ride horses, the Tellingtons moved to the States and settled in California. There Went taught math at Chadwick, a small private prep school in Rolling Hills, outside Los Angeles. The school desperately needed an eighth-grade social studies teacher and prevailed upon Linda to teach that class, even though she had neither a teaching degree nor classroom teaching experience. But she had been a riding instructor since she was thirteen and she quickly took to teaching. Giving presentations to groups large and small was never a problem; it was the one-on-one communication that confounded her. Naturally shy and reserved, she was intimidated by her commanding husband and his well-educated comrades.

After four years of teaching at Chadwick, she and Went started buying and selling Thoroughbreds. The two collaborated in running a breeding farm with ninety Thoroughbred broodmares, four stallions, and twenty Arabians.

The Tellingtons' Equine Business

In the early 1960s the Tellingtons ran a summer camp for children on a 400-acre ranch on the California coast at San Luis Obispo. While there a woman asked them to give her riding lessons; she had been referred by one of show jumper Anne Kursinski's top instructors (see Anne's chapter). Adult students were rare in those days. Linda demurred, but the woman talked her into it. The Tellingtons hadn't considered specializing in training adults. Working with adults changed Linda's life.

"I remember my first adult student at Chadwick in 1961," Linda says. "It was an airline pilot and he wanted to learn to ride, so I put him on a horse and I taught him — elbows in, heels down. That's what they taught in the cavalry. He went around the ring a couple times. He stopped and said, 'Why are you doing this?' I had no idea why. I went home and asked my husband. I figured he had a cavalry officer background. He knows everything. He gave me a long lecture on why and he didn't say a thing. I can remember that moment like yesterday. That's when I started wanting to know why."

In seeking the reasons behind the familiar rules, Linda explored the idea of establishing a center of gravity in your body to make it easier for the rider and the horse. Sally Swift (see Sally's chapter) was beginning to write about these topics and her work informed Linda's. Based on her experience and what she learned from others, Linda began to develop her own methods.

The Tellingtons' next adventure, in 1964, was the development of an innovative equine facility, the Pacific Coast Equestrian Research Farm and School of Horsemanship, in Badger, California, southeast of Fresno. The Tellingtons had about forty-five horses of all ages, including Thoroughbreds, Hungarians, Morgans, and Quarter Horses, and they bred their own horses as well. During its ten years of operation, the school drew students from nine countries and thirty-six states. Lucile Bump, Sally Swift's protegee (See Sally's chapter) was a student of Linda's in those days.

The school offered a nine-month residential instructor-training program for adult riders. Nowhere else could students between the ages of eighteen and twenty, each of whom had to have at least ten years of riding experience, receive such intensive training in horsemanship. Students learned a basic balance seat, but were expected to master a variety of equitation styles. To graduate as an instructor, they had to score at least 50-percent in a second-level dressage test, to complete a 100-mile endurance race, to show successfully in hunter and western pleasure classes, and to compete in combined training. They had to jump three feet on a cross-country course, bareback, and start a young horse. In addition to working with horses, students attended cultural events in the city, and a dress code was in effect at mealtime; one did not come to dinner in one's barn clothes!

The goal was to turn out riding teachers who could teach with compassion and skill, giving priority to the physical, mental, and spiritual well-being of horses and students. The Tellingtons' mantra was "observation," observation of self, one's body, and, especially, observation of the horses' reactions. The couple operated as a team. Went did the organizing and acted as the creative force behind their teaching and research; Linda was the instructor, the one who valued and maintained relationships with clients, students, and horses.

The school's approach was different from anything offered in either European or North American training barns. Says Linda, "Our interest was in turning out instructors who like people as much as horses, because in the horse world before Sally Swift, it was just a question of the teacher standing in the middle of the ring yelling to their students. Some of them threw horse manure at their students. You want to learn, why are you being yelled at?"

In other ways, too, Wentworth Tellington was "way ahead of his time," says Linda. He developed a horse product from dried sea kelp that sold all over the country. He also created natural vitamin and mineral products to keep horses healthy and athletic. He and Linda conducted clinical studies on the differences between methods of worming horses. They studied the effects of apple-cider vinegar — an old New England remedy for fly control — by counting the number of times the horses swished their tails. They studied alternatives to cribbing straps, which can create headaches and pain for the horse. An excellent writer, Went wrote up their research findings for various equestrian magazines. They did a monthly column, "Let's Go," and published a research letter that went out to subscribers in twenty countries. Their first book, *Massage and Physical Therapy for the Athletic Horse*, was published in 1965, based on what Linda had learned from her grandfather, Will Caywood. The Tellingtons became widely known in the horse field for their expertise.

Though she had branched out into teaching, training horses, and equine research, Linda still took competition seriously. She finished in the top ten in the Tevis Cup, the famous hundred-mile endurance race and weeks later set a record in the Jim Shoulders race with her mare Bint Gulida. Not only did they finish six hours ahead of the next pair, they won the award for best-conditioned horse. Bint Gulida went on to become an outstanding broodmare, producing top endurance mounts. While continuing her own show ring success, Linda added an American Horse Show Association judge's card to her credentials and began judging English and Western pleasure classes.

After a local paper featured an in-depth article about their work, the Tellingtons were asked by a California state agency to develop a program for disabled young people between ages fifteen and twenty-one; the purpose of the program was to help prepare the participants for the work world. In response, the Tellingtons developed one of the country's first therapeutic riding programs. Linda experimented successfully with teaching these young people to ride bareback. Now therapeutic riding is a big industry and its benefits well established, but back then only a few farsighted people realized how working with horses could help people of various backgrounds and abilities to develop confidence, self-esteem, physical coordination, and a sense of responsibility.

During this period, inspired by the book the old former cavalry officer had given her years before at Briarcrest and by the influence of her grandfather, Linda developed a system of starting young horses by ground-driving them first, teaching them to walk, trot, canter, turn, and stop before a saddle was put on them. "It was completely safe — anybody could do it," Linda says now. "That was one of the beauties. You didn't have to have experience. You didn't have to have the skill to chase them around a round pen, where you had to be good with your timing and signals to get the horse to understand. We found we could do it so much easier."

Linda's Marital Troubles

During these years of intense creativity and productivity for both Tellingtons, Went's alcoholism became more and more evident. Linda continued to admire his intellect and his capacity to create and organize innovative projects, but she also learned to avoid him after three o'clock in the afternoon. His personality, always dominant and sometimes domineering, veered toward overt abusiveness, first mental and later physical. With continuous heavy exposure to alcohol, Went became erratic. Linda never knew if a simple question would elicit a civil response or an explosion. He would yell at students or staff for picayune things. Once he lashed out at the school cook in public for serving pears instead of peaches. Linda was horrified.

In 1972, when Linda was thirty-five, Went suddenly left the house; Linda thinks he meant to teach her a lesson. After many years of submitting to his erratic moods, she had begun to stand up to him, more often to protect others from his wrath than to protect herself. She remembers: "What happened was a couple of times he got really mad at me because I wouldn't tell him what student had said something if they were unhappy with him or the program. I simply wouldn't tell him who it was because I knew he would take it out on them. He was sitting there chopping wood at the fireplace in our living room. I remember turning around and walking out. I'm sure the hair on the back of my head was standing up because I thought I was going to get the axe on the back of my head. He threw a whiskey glass at me so hard that it hit an oak bench and made a dent."

Did Went ever hurt her physically? "He tried," she says with a wry laugh. "But I'm not very hurtable. You know where he really hurt me as a human being was that in front of other people he'd be really nice and then when we were alone, he'd rip me up one side and down the other. It's so funny, I've managed to blank out a lot of that stuff. Just see the positive in the whole experience." Despite his escalating verbal and physical violence over the years, Linda didn't consider leaving him. But when he walked out, a large part of her was relieved to have him gone. It confirmed the wisdom of her earlier decision not to have children with Went. He already had two grown children from whom he was estranged, and she didn't see any signs that his aptitude for fatherhood had changed.

In trying to keep the marriage and the business partnership together, Linda tapped into some spiritual strength of her own. Recounting one incident, she says, "What happened one time, and this is really significant in my life ... He was sleeping with another woman and I was boo-hooing and carrying on. I was probably thirty. I decided I needed some help from a book. I reached up and pulled out *The Prophet* by Gibran and read 'The self same well from which your sorrows flow, will also flow your joy.' I thought, Yes! Someday this well will be so deep. But it will be filled with joy. So anytime something happened to me that was difficult, I just thought about that. It's totally true."

The only person in whom Linda confided about her husband's behavior was her dear friend and mentor Margit Bessenyey, who happened to be a wealthy Hungarian countess. Countess Margit, twenty years Linda's senior, had taken the younger woman under her wing. Starting in 1964, Margit had a dozen horses in training with the Tellingtons for as long as two years at a time. Their relationship continued until Margit died. The two women would talk for an hour every morning so that Margit could hear stories about her beloved horses. She also got occasional updates about Went's abusiveness.

When Went walked out, Margit said, "Why don't you divorce him?" Linda had never considered it before. She hadn't told her family about his abuse either, but they knew, because Linda's younger sister Robyn often witnessed the scenes while at the stable. When Linda finally told her family, her mother exclaimed, "Oh, dear, thank God, finally!"

Years later, Went shot himself, a perfect ending for a cavalry officer who never wanted to live in an old age home. Linda remained in close contact with him until the last month of his life. But his departure from both the marriage and their business had freed her up to become her own person.

Linda ended this chapter of her life with a flourish. Margit Bessenyey urged her to find another place to live and work, and with Margit's financial help, Linda bought a beautiful barn in Los Altos Hills in northern California. She started with twenty horses and soon established her own business — a feat she never imagined she could manage without Went's expertise.

Soon she remarried. Her second husband, Rich Jones, was much younger than she. He was an amateur athlete whom Linda met through her association with the Los Altos Hunt Club. The marriage did not last long.

Self-Exploration Led to New Adventures

Once she moved to Los Altos Hills, Linda had an epiphany. Up on a mountaintop during a three-day event, in 102-degree heat, responsible for horses, vans, and students, she asked herself what she wanted to do with her life. Thanks to the kindness of Margit Bessenyey, she had some breathing room to figure it out.

Linda began to do some self-exploration. She spent time at Esalen Institute and got interested in Alexander Technique, Gestalt, and other self-awareness methods. She discovered Findhorn, on the northern coast of Scotland, run by Peter and Eileen Caddy, who wrote books about spirituality. "I had this strong feeling after Esalen that my life was not just about horses," she says. "I was discouraged from what I was seeing in the horse business because we had a way of being with horses that was really respectful and kind. It worked, made people feel good about themselves when they were with horses. What I saw around me was just the same old thing, beat the horses up, make them do what you want them to do. Not honoring them as our teachers at all." That wasn't what she wanted to do, but she wasn't clear how to implement her ideas.

She sat down with the dean at the University of California at Santa Cruz, where she had taught adult horsemanship courses. He said, "You are already very successful. I think you should go out in the world and see what finds you. You know what you want to do. Go out and find it." She decided to take two years off and "go wherever the wind took me."

She went to visit Ursula Brun, a German friend who wanted her to train a group of horses for a demonstration at Equitana, the huge European equestrian exposition. Ursula published a magazine called *Free Time in the Saddle*. She knew about the Tellingtons because of their magazine articles and had spent time with them in California. She asked Linda to "do something spectacular to show the American style of riding." As Linda explains it: "Back in 1969, we had taken four Hungarians [horses] and had toured the United States and given an exhibition of two stallions, a mare, and a gelding with no bridles. A jumping drill. People thought it was great. I did that for Equitana in Germany and they went crazy. They couldn't believe we could ride a horse with nothing on their head. And we did it without saddles. No one did that in Germany in those days. Ursula Bruns took our style of riding without bridles and made it into the only course in the world for adult riders to learn in eleven days how to ride at the walk, trot, and canter and jump with no bridle."

After the sensational show at Equitana, Ursula insisted that Linda write down her methods. This was the first step on Linda's journey toward creating books and videos about TTEAM.

The Idea of Tellington T-Touch Started With Feldenkrais Training

At about the same time, she enrolled in the first American based four-year Feldenkrais training with Dr. Moshe Feldenkrais himself at the Humanistic Psychology Institute in California. She had done a workshop with Ilana Rubenfeld in Alexander Technique and Feldenkrais, and in only one hour it had dramatically changed her riding. She was flabbergasted. She thought she could use what she learned in the Feldenkrais training to enhance the athleticism of her riding students as well.

Instead, she found the training "completely life-changing." Moshe Feldenkrais taught Linda something that made a huge impact on her. The message was that it is possible for anyone to learn from gentle, non-habitual movements that will activate new neural pathways and new brain cells. This is the essence of the Feldenkrais method.

Linda mused: "If that's true for humans, it's true for a horse. What can I do with the horse that would be a non-habitual movement? One that they couldn't do themselves, that would activate new connections to the brain so that they would learn how to learn faster?" Linda experimented with a sixteen-year-old broodmare from a ranch in Montana. The horse had never been ridden. She started moving the horse's lips, her ears, her chin. After forty-five minutes, the horse was totally relaxed. The next day the owner said she didn't know what Linda had done, but the mare was easy to catch for the first time. She came right to the gate. She didn't dive for her food when she got into her stall.

"I had already been working on horses' bodies for years from the point of view of massage and helping the horse to recover faster after endurance riding or racing or horse shows," Linda says now, reflecting on those key early experiences.

In 1961, when he was eighty-two, her grandfather Will Caywood had spent time with the Tellingtons. He showed them the massage techniques he had used working with the tsar's horses in Russia in the early years of the twentieth century. An Austrian count had hired him to go to Moscow to race horses; he had stayed on to train, becoming the leading race trainer by 1905. He attributed his success to his use of massage.

Nevertheless, Linda continues, "it never crossed my mind that you could change the behavior of a horse by working on the body. What I found with the Feldenkrais philosophy of non-habitual movement is that a horse would want to learn and be totally cooperative in a matter of minutes without running them around, tiring them out, showing them who's boss, dominating the horse, none of that. It was such a beautiful way of engaging the horse in a way that was joyful to them as well as to the person."

This discovery launched Linda's personal mission: to work with horses — and, eventually, other animals and humans — in such a way that created a partnership between horse and human, and a new way for the horse to experience its own body. Horses are prey animals, and much of their instinctive behavior, including aggressiveness, is rooted in fear. Linda's approach was not to punish the horse for being fearful but to let the horse know what she expected and to find out where the fear was coming from. Was it from physical pain, or from a new situation, or from a previous bad experience? This philosophy was revolutionary in those days.

By the late 1970s, Linda was heavily involved in exploring the implications of moving horses' bodies in these non-habitual ways; she integrated what she was learning with the ground-driving exercises that she had been doing for years. Later it became known as the *Playground for Higher Learning* and was incorporated into her TTEAM approach.

She describes an example of the Playground technique: "I took five riders who were absolute amateurs. I took twenty horses that were sent by trainers, vets, and owners who had given up on them and then I put them through movements and ground obstacles. There were a couple of runaways, horses that were so spooky that the riders were always getting thrown off or horses that were really stiff. One that was sent by a vet had a neurological dysfunction that made it throw its head so badly that the rider would fall down. Another was dangerous; he'd bolt and run away. We took all these horses and put them through the exact same program. Seventeen of the twenty horses came around completely. Three did not respond well enough."

While Linda was exploring how to spend the rest of her life, she decided to visit Russia, where her grandfather had ridden and trained racehorses in the early 1900s. When they passed the Hippodrome in Moscow, Linda told her Soviet Intourist guide that her grandfather had raced horses there for the tsar. It turned out that the guide was an amateur riding instructor at the Hippodrome! She immediately offered to set up a meeting so that Linda could demonstrate her work with horses. As a result, Linda returned to the Soviet Union as a citizen ambassador ten times between 1984 and 1987 to teach TTouch to the Olympic dressage and show jumping teams and to train equine veterinarians as well as zoo managers.

Research on Inter-Species Communication

In the course for vets, they compared horses who had had the experience of TTouch with a control group of those who had not; they analyzed the cortisol level in blood samples and found a significant reduction in those who had been exposed to her methods. This furthered her desire to test the effect of her methods in a scientific way, an interest that culminated much later, in 2008, in her honorary doctorate from Wisdom University and her chairmanship of the Institute for InterSpecies Communication. The mission of the Institute is to encourage research to explore the impact of human communications on other species and its effect on the health of human beings.

Going to Russia back in the 1980s was the catalyst for yet another program. "That's how my whole Animal Ambassador program started," Linda says. "What I found was that everywhere I went, when I talked to Russians about animals, they would completely open up. It's not only that we were the ambassadors for the animals, but the animals were our ambassadors." She has since developed the nonprofit organization, Animal Ambassadors International, to support children in working with animals to "enhance understanding, compassion and quality of life for both humans and animals." When Linda works with horses or companion animals, she recalls something she learned during her Feldenkrais training, from the book *Man and His Nature*, by Sir Charles Sherrington, a researcher and physician. As she recalls it, he had written something like this: "Isn't the body a wonder? We could cut out several inches of nerve and most of the time those two ends would grow back together. How can that be possible? Very simple, because every cell in our body knows its function within the body and its function within the universe."

"Cells, remember your potential for functioning." She repeats, then continues: "And that's how I started thinking of my work with humans and with horses. I began thinking of the body as a collection of cells. The idea of very gently reminding the cells of their potential for perfection and, of course, what happens is the body heals itself. The body remembers. The beauty of it is that a person can use it on their animals, but they can also use it on themselves. It's not just to make the animal feel better, but it affects their ability to perform and affects behavior and relationship with people. It deepens the bond. It's something that people can do for their animals." This thinking clarified the scientific origins of her TTouch methods.

In 1995 Linda and her staff started to conduct a two-year training for companion animals, such as dogs and cats, in sites all over the world, in Germany, Austria, South Africa, and Canada. They've expanded their system to include training practitioners, mostly physical therapists, to translate this method to working with humans. She and her co-author published a book called *Tellington T-Touch for the Health Care Professional: A Practical Guide for Humans*. She feels validated by seeing so many people all over the world having such good outcomes with all kinds of creatures, animal and human. It verifies her spiritual sense of connection to animals and people, which began back on her family farm in Western Canada.

After being single for twenty-five years, Linda is happily married to Roland Kleger, a longtime friend and former student; they make their home

Linda At Home On The Big Island, HI

on the Big Island of Hawaii, where Roland runs the Animal Ambassadors program. Although Linda has come a long way from the shy Canadian girl who could "stick on anything," she still sees horses as giving us the "gift of inspiration." She loves being around them, loves "their smell, their snuffles and their language. One of the most favorite times with horses is just being in the barn at night, after feeding time, quiet. My basic concept is being able to make a difference here on the planet and serve a higher source. I think that's what brings happiness to me."

At seventy-one, Linda, a natural ambassador for aging inspirationally, says, "I'm just getting started. I've never had more clarity, drive, health, or intent as I do now."

Valerie Kanavy

World Champion Endurance Rider

© 1993 Genie Stewart-Spears *Valerie Riding Cash*

"I'm sure my name will be remembered in the sport of endurance because of what I've accomplished. But the reality is I'm not saving the world. I'm racing horses. What is important to me is that I be remembered as being a good person who had a positive impact on those around me."

Endurance riding is among the most demanding equestrian sports for both horse and rider. In a typical ride, 50, 75, or even 100 miles of demanding terrain must be covered in a day; two- and three-day rides may cover up to 150 miles. Endurance riding imposes the strictest monitoring of horse welfare of any form of equestrian competition. All equine competitors must be vetted before they are allowed to start, then at regular checkpoints along the way the horse's vital signs are checked and must be within prescribed limits before he's allowed to continue. The endurance horse must be in peak physical and mental condition; the award given for the best-conditioned horse at each ride is widely considered as important as winning.

The successful endurance rider is a master strategist who knows intimately both the capabilities of the horse and the demands of the course. Despite, or more likely because of, the challenges, endurance riding is increasing in popularity not only in the United States but abroad as well. Since 1993 endurance riding has been an approved discipline of the U.S. Equestrian Federation (USEF), which now sponsors teams in world competition. The American Endurance Ride Conference sanctions competitions in the U.S. and Canada and is an affiliate organization of the USEF.

Valerie Kanavy, two-time World Endurance gold medalist, silver medalist, multiple champion and winner of countless rides, is among the most successful and respected endurance riders in North America. In January 2009, Valerie was honored with the Maggy Price Endurance Excellence Award, which honors the athlete who has earned the most points in ranking trials during the past year.

What Is a 100 Mile Endurance Race Like?

Here's how Valerie describes a typical endurance competition. For a 100-mile race, riders may tack up before dawn. The day before, each horse will have been examined by a veterinarian for soundness and fitness; those that don't pass aren't allowed to start. In an unfamiliar place, surrounded by horses they don't know, the horses are usually keyed up.

The excitement continues into the first miles. Horses are herd animals and moving at speed with other horses can lead to an exuberance that's hard to control. It's important, Valerie emphasizes, that a horse not fritter away too much energy at this stage. Depending on the terrain and the temperature, the pace can range from 7 or 8 miles per hour up to 15, with the average somewhere around 10. Riders want to control the speed at first and keep a steady pace, so that they'll "have enough gas in the tank," as Valerie puts it, to complete the ride.

Riders are timed in at each checkpoint. The clock doesn't stop until the horse's pulse drops to 64. To get the pulse down as fast as possible, people may, if the weather is warm enough, put water on the big blood vessels to relax the horse and thus bring the pulse rate down. In cold weather this doesn't work because cold water will raise the pulse instead. For a fit horse who has been sensibly ridden and who isn't overexcited, it generally takes only two to five minutes to get the metabolic rates to a suitable place. At that point the rider and horse move into the vet area for examination.

The veterinarian verifies that the pulse is down. Then the horse is trotted in hand 125 feet out and back, to check for lameness. The vet is concerned about the possibility of dehydration on such long and strenuous rides. To test for that, the vet pinches a fold of flesh to see how long it takes for the skin to smooth out. Another way of measuring dehydration is to measure the capillary refill; this is a measure of the ability of the horse to pump blood to the small vessels in the mouth. The vet measures how long it takes the pink color to reappear after applying pressure to the gum. The horse is then checked to make sure the saddle is fitting and not causing any soreness in the back and examined for heat in the legs that might indicate lameness. Finally the horse is given a pass or fail score. A "fail" means the horse is disqualified. Then the horses are fed and watered, and the riders get a snack.

To help out at the checkpoints, Valerie usually takes a crew along with her — other competitors who can anticipate what she needs and not get in the way. She's had the experience of working with local crew who didn't know what they were doing and put her and her horse in jeopardy. Since then, she uses her own crew.

Having trained as a runner herself, she knows that running uphill is harder than running downhill. She's astute enough on a horse to know when he's giving maximum effort, as opposed to working within his capacities. When you're racing long distances, you constantly have to judge to what extent the horse is working at a level that will enable him to have the energy to "go the distance," Valerie explains. How well he's been trained and innate athleticism are two variables that affect any horse competitor's endurance.

Valerie's Childhood Wouldn't Suggest She'd Be a World Champion

When I met Valerie Kanavy, she looked the part of a Victorian lady, elegant in a floor length dress with a bustle, long gloves, and a hat with a wide brim. She had just returned from a costumed event to benefit a handicapped riding organization near her Florida home. Petite, blond, and physically restrained by her ornate garb, she didn't exactly look like a highly disciplined athlete who has competed all over the world. But that's exactly what she is.

Where did Valerie's passion for horses come from? That's a mystery. The oldest of six children, she was not exposed to horses or even Westerns as a youngster. Her family didn't have a TV; her working-class parents didn't know anything about horses — her mother, she remembers, was downright afraid of them — and they didn't have the means to provide lessons. Yet Valerie's fascination with horses had taken root before she started school. According to family lore, she said "horse" before she said "Mommy" or "Daddy." Her earliest years were spent in a suburban subdivision in Fresno, California. When she was seven, the family relocated to Wichita, Kansas. Both her parents, however, were originally from upstate New York, where an uncle ran a big dairy farm. Valerie loved it. Her uncle, she remembers, "worked the cows and had some hired hands. I used to die to be out on the farms. Even though there were no horses, there was still a farm. So I always had that thing somewhere in my blood."

In Kansas as in California, Valerie's family lived in suburbia, far from horse pastures or stables. The goal of riding was rarely far from Valerie's mind, however. While still in elementary school, she started a newspaper route, baby sat, did odd jobs, and saved her money. By age eleven, she had enough money to buy herself a gray mare, probably a Quarter Horse cross, for $150. From then on the 35 cents an hour she made baby sitting and the money from her paper route went toward paying the $35 a month board. "There was no extra money for lessons," she says, and besides, "I don't know who I would have taken lessons with. I was just a kid in the backyard."

As a young child, while still in California, Valerie contracted such a serious case of polio that she refers to her recovery as "one of those miracle cases." As far as she knows, she has had no residual effects from the disease, although she thinks about it when she's exceedingly tired for no apparent reason.

In Wichita, Valerie was an active, athletic child who excelled at swimming. Her suburban subdivision had a swim club in the summer; she swam on the boys' team as well as the girls' because there weren't enough boys competing. She also played tennis and baseball. Horses, however, were number one. Her bemused parents could not offer financial support, but they didn't stand in her way either. Being a suburban kid, she didn't have horsey friends, but joined 4-H, so was introduced to local horse shows there.

The day she turned sixteen and could get a driver's license, she purchased a trailer she could take to horse shows. "I can't believe I did that," she says now. "A kid driving a horse trailer ... Ignorance is bliss. If you don't know what you don't know, then you think you know. You just do it." Valerie remembers a "big ole grey Studebaker" that her father found for her, but it's hard to imagine how that vehicle could pull a trailer and horse.

Valerie was considerably less passionate about school than she was about horses. As a youngster she attended Catholic school, then she transferred to the public school for middle and high school. "School wasn't a minus, nor was it a big plus," she says now. "It just was." She enjoyed the friendships she made there, however. After graduating from high school, Valerie went to Kansas State College in Pittsburgh, Kansas, even though academic pursuits weren't her major interest. Somehow, she managed to take her horse with her. Living in a dorm, her parents gave her money for meals; she used it to feed her horse as well as herself. "It was a crazy thing," she admits.

At first her horse lived at a nearby farm. That barn turned out to be an unwise decision. Seems that some of the guys would be out drinking, daring one another to catch and ride her horse, even though they didn't know anything about horses. When their games didn't work out to their liking, they could become abusive toward her animal. She learned the hard way that she couldn't keep her horse with her at school. Valerie met her husband-to-be, Larry Kanavy, at school and through him she found a more suitable home for her horse. But her college career was short-lived, because she didn't "buckle down and study," she admits. She moved back to Wichita and went to work in a clothing store.

She also sold her horse because none of her equestrian activities had really hooked her. She had done some showing in Western classes like barrel racing and a little Quarter Horse racing, but without instruction or a trainer her progress was limited. What was the point? To improve her job prospects, she studied to be an operating room technician and worked in a hospital OR for a short time.

Marriage and Moving East to Horse Country

At the age of twenty-one, Valerie married Larry Kanavy. The couple moved to Pennsylvania, where Larry had a job in the building industry. Chester County, where the young couple eventually settled, is horse country. There Valerie met Michele Scofield, the wife of her husband's co-worker, a woman who rode and hunted. Michele invited Valerie to ride with her. Valerie was in totally new territory; she made it up as she went along. "I was riding by the seat of my pants, because I had ridden so much bareback," she recalls. "I had never been in an English saddle and was able to jump right over this stuff. Beginner's luck, I guess. The horse did it, I sat on it." Because she stayed on the horse, jumping over some natural fences on the trail, she impressed her new friend enough to offer to take her fox hunting.

What a revelation! In the saddle all day long, riding over fences, Valerie remembers thinking to herself, "'Oh my gosh, now I know what a horse is for!' This was nothing like anything I'd ever done out West. And it was fast. It felt like it took some skill. I really loved it, and from that point on, I was back into horses, because now I had something I could do with the horse that's really fun."

Ready for another horse of her own, Valerie purchased her first Arabian, a yearling, because she could only afford a young horse. She also had a small quarter horse mare she had purchased in Kansas and rode her until the Arab was old enough to be mounted. Soon she realized that for a horse to perform well on hunts and other rigorous all-day rides, he has to be in excellent condition — and that conditioning a horse is the rider's responsibility. This hadn't occurred to her back in her Wichita days when she'd hop on a horse bareback and just go, go, go. She had assumed that horses were big, strong animals that were naturally capable of strenuous activity, and that horses succeeded in top competitions like the

Kentucky Derby because they were genetically superior. Back in her swimming days, she had trained conscientiously to build up her own speed and stamina. Horses worked the same way, she finally surmised! They had to train just as much as humans to become fit for rigorous physical activities.

Jogging and physical fitness were then becoming popular in the United States. Valerie had three children in rapid succession, Trevon, Danielle, and Timmy — at one point all three were in diapers at the same time — and between pregnancies she jogged. While pregnant with Trevon, she rode until her sixth month, then she was sidelined by a "spreading pelvis," caused by pregnancy-related hormone changes. She translated what she learned about keeping herself fit into conditioning her horses, the Arab when he got old enough, and the quarter horse. She rode them daily with the express purpose of strengthening them for the hunt. But, lacking a mentor or instructor to help her with her own form or with conditioning exercises for her horses, she had to make it up as she went along. Then her young Arabian "the one", she had been doing point-to-point races and fox hunting with, went lame. "I thought I was building Super Horse," Valerie says. Her horse's lameness was a rude surprise — and a wake-up call.

Over the hill from the Kanavys lived Bob MacBurney, an elderly horseman who ran a private stable for the local huntsmaster. MacBurney taught her not only how to recognize and treat lameness but how to keep a horse sound. He demonstrated the importance of proper shoeing for a hardworking performance horse. Valerie learned belatedly that she hadn't conditioned her horse appropriately for the work she was asking her to do. "I was hooked into the game," she says. She wanted to learn more. And she's challenged herself ever since to keep up with the latest in horse conditioning techniques.

With three small children at home, "I was up to my eyeballs," Valerie recalls. The horses became an escape from changing diapers. Whenever she had time and could get local teenage baby sitters, she'd go off on horseback. At that time, her spouse was not a house-husband; he was out working long hours, building up a business that ultimately supported the family well.

Valerie Discovers the Sport of Endurance Racing

In 1972, Mr. MacBurney introduced her to a local woman who told her about the Tevis Cup, the famous endurance ride that covers 100 miles from

Tahoe to Auburn, California. The top finishers often cover the daunting distance in less than fourteen hours. Valerie was intrigued. That year, her new friend took her to her first local competition to start to train for the more challenging Tevis. Valerie entered the 25-mile division — and won. In her next ride, a couple of months later, her horse was the top-finishing Arabian and the pair placed third overall.

Arabs are especially suited to long-distance riding, having been originally bred by desert nomads to cover long miles without water or much nourishment. Since they are lightweight, lean, and possessed of a large lung capacity, the well-conditioned Arab can travel a long time without tiring. The desert horses customarily lived in close quarters with humans, and plenty of Arabian enthusiasts will swear that they picked up some human qualities in the process! "They are super-responsive," she said. "They have emotions, actions, and opinions." You can even, she swore, "have conversations with them ... which makes it a whole bunch more fun!"

By then Larry Kanavy knew that endurance riding was going to be Valerie's life passion. He decided to learn to ride as well. The sport of endurance riding was in its infancy in the early 1970s, so the Kanavys were among the first to compete on the East coast. She did most of the day-to-day training and conditioning of the horses, then she and Larry competed together. From the beginning they were fairly successful at the local endurance rides. But, it wasn't until she had a freak accident that they really committed to going to the Tevis.

"I was out fox hunting one New Year's Day," Valerie remembers, "and my husband was watching from the car with the kids, and the horse took off, lost his balance, and went down on the pavement. His feet went out from under him. I ended up lying in the middle of the road with my feet twitching and my eyes all back in my head, unconscious and with a concussion ... From that point on, instead of thinking that someday we will go do the Tevis, we decided we would start doing those things, because you never knew what was going to happen tomorrow."

At that time, their friends, the veterinarian Dr. Matthew Mackay-Smith and his wife, Winkie, had been to the Tevis and were planning another trip. The Kanavys decided to join them. Valerie had an International Scout and a 2-horse trailer, which carried the horses she and Larry were going to ride. She deposited the three kids at her family's home in Kansas and then met

The Kanavys With 3 Kings

up with the Mackay-Smiths and caravanned out to California, with a little delay because of car trouble due to hauling the trailer over mountains in high altitude. Larry flew out and was waiting for them. She remembers the reception they got at Tevis.

"We were pretty tired when we arrived. I remember a big gentleman, Wentworth Tellington [Linda Tellington-Jones' ex- husband], who met us. His first question was 'What made us think we were horsemen enough to be able to ride the Tevis?' We had come a long way and I was exhausted. It was really a slap in the face. I felt like crying – it made Larry fighting mad!"

Valerie remembers starting the ride in a ski lodge parking lot. Lots of horse trailers were lined up side by side with horses tied to them, standing on gravel. They started the horses in groups of ten. You drew numbers for your group. Naturally, the four of them wanted to ride together and share the ride they had come so far to experience. But, no, they were not allowed to ride together because they hadn't picked the right numbers to do so. "Anyone who even attempted to trade numbers or change groups would be disqualified," they were told. "We felt like unwelcome guests... It was the most unfriendly ride management we had ever encountered." She was in one of the last groups and succeeded in catching up to her husband and friends about thirty miles into the event. What she remembers other than the dictatorial nature of the management, led by Went Tellington, was that they had to travel in a single lane trail, there was so much dust you could not see below your horse's shoulder and there was no opportunity to race because you couldn't pass other horse and rider pairs. "I'm afraid the Tevis holds no magic for me," says Val.

Now the Tevis Cup is so popular that it attracts as many as 250 horses. With such a big crowd, the competitors might be "seeded" at the start, or sent off in smaller groups, as they were in the Kanavy's ordeal in the 1970s. "They call the Tevis 'the tourist ride,'" Valerie says, "because everybody's heard of it. Many of them are there to do it in less than twenty-four hours. They're not racing the course. They're just challenged by it, much like people who do marathons. You'll have your class of real runners who are racing the marathon, then you'll have people who have trained quite a bit who are going for best time, and then you have the majority who have trained, but are trying to go for the accomplishment of being able to do a marathon."

Years later after competing in Leesburg, Virginia, the Kanavys decided they would eventually move there. Suburbia was encroaching on their cherished trails in Pennsylvania; they wanted to be near government-protected land where they could continue to ride and train their horses right from their back yard. They settled in Fort Valley, Virginia, near the George Washington National Forest in the Shenandoah Valley.

Looking Toward International Competition

In 1992, Larry encouraged Valerie to try for a place on the new U.S. squad for the 1994 World Championship. In order to be considered for international competition, she needed to have a consistent record on one horse. She had her doubts about challenging herself in the international arena. What if she failed?

In the early days of competing internationally, it was not very different from competing in the States. There was more "pomp and circumstance," tighter vet controls, and courses were more carefully measured. What has made a difference over the years of endurance competitions is the emerging professionalism in the sport.

In the US, there is a culture of wanting to finish a race, rather than race it. "It's the American endurance rider mentality," Valerie explains. "Endurance in the US has risen from the back yard horse owner-rider. Quite a distance from professional horsemen with many prejudicial views toward professionals."

In other parts of the world, unlike the American viewpoint, the sport is very professional, utilizing full time trainers, expensive horses, and the serious commitment of competitors. It's winning, not just completing the course that's at the heart of international competition. So, it's much more challenging and also exhilarating to compete. Riders utilize all the scientific knowledge that they can apply to training their endurance horses in order to win. Winners are respected by peers and supported financially by their governments. In contrast, the AERC (the American Endurance Riding Conference) is focused more on the number of races and miles covered, rather than on winning. It wasn't until 1994 that the USET funded the International endurance event, although Americans had participated in international events before that.

At the time that Valerie started to train for international events, she had two Arabian horses in training. One was bought by Italians and went on to become the number one endurance horse in Europe. She kept the other, Pieraz. She spent the next year getting "Cash," as Pieraz was called in the barn, ready for higher-level competition. They competed in the 1993 North American Championship in Calgary and finished sixth, even though Cash had been sick a few days before. But then he went lame; Valerie was devastated. It was Larry who persuaded her to try again. He offered to take her wherever she needed to go to compete. For many endurance riders in the US, the mantra is "To finish is to win," but Larry told Valerie, "Stop riding to finish! Ride to win!" which was more akin to what international competitors believed in. She took up the challenge.

Once Cash was sound again, he and Valerie went on to win seven of the eight 100-mile rides they entered, which put them in a good position to be chosen to compete internationally. They were chosen to ride the 1994 World Endurance Championship in the Hague, the Netherlands. She won the individual gold medal. Don't forget... Valerie had never had a lesson. She was entirely self-taught. And here she was winning on the competitive international stage. In 1996 in Kansas, she took home the silver; the winner, by a narrow margin, was her daughter, Danielle, who by this time was competing right next to her mother. Valerie earned her second gold medal in 1998 in Dubai on High Winds Jedi. She told an interviewer that this particular win "was tremendously satisfying as it had the largest representation of competitors from throughout the world ... To be able to compete with such caliber and numbers was a real thrill. It was the greatest test for me." Success at the highest levels makes you try harder, she says. You're continually motivated "to figure out how to do something better, how to make it more efficient, to train better, to make better electrolytes, to give the horses better feed."

Valerie reached the upper echelons of her sport with no formal training, but at every step of the way she was listening, learning, looking for what she needed to know. The more I learned, the more I did, the more I picked people's brains," she says. "If I had a problem, I would figure out how to solve it or whom I could get the information from that could solve it for me. There's a lot of resources out there."

A Life-Long Equestrienne Learner

In the mid-1990s, already a World Cup gold medalist, she started working with Donna Snyder-Smith, who has become Valerie's mentor and trainer. Snyder-Smith trained in dressage from the time she was a little girl in Germany. When her family moved back to the United States, she became an advocate of Sally Swift's *Centered Riding* (see Sally's chapter), which she believed made it easier to teach dressage. From Sally she learned how the horse's body and the rider's body work best, both independently and in partnership. Snyder-Smith went on to publish several books, including *The Complete Guide to Endurance Riding and Competition*. In 2007 she was named one of the fifty best riding instructors in the U.S. From her Valerie has learned much about balance, control, and communication with the horse.

"I had a horse that was very powerful, but when I got on him, there was no power from back in the engine," Valerie recalls. "I didn't know how to activate it, and all of a sudden I realized I'd just been a passenger sitting on him. I didn't actually know how to use seat and legs and hands. That was a big change. You could have two lifetimes and still not learn everything. I was pretty successful just doing what I was doing, but then all of a sudden I ran into a horse that required something different, and had to figure it out. A big eye-opener." Snyder-Smith taught her to ride better, not just "by the seat of my pants," and "how to use gymnastic exercises to boost the training effects" on her horses.

In addition to seeking out ways to improve her training methods, Valerie is always interested in the newest technology and equipment. She works hard to reduce any performance-related injuries or conditions that the horses face. She uses a heart rate monitor, for instance, to gauge the heart rate of the horse she's training. She likes to make sure that her horse is not running at an anaerobic rate too long, because this causes an oxygen deficiency, which can lead to long-term problems. If the horse is traveling too fast for his conditioning, then she knows about it and can adjust the pace. She might use a bio-scan machine to identify which muscles are being overused. Then she can treat them with an infrared cold laser to alleviate soreness.

Daughter Danielle, a nurse, is partly responsible for her mother's interest in veterinary technology. Danielle is familiar with equine physiology, and she keeps up with the latest research. The two have competed together in races around the world. They make a good team. They work out their course strategies together. On the trail, they keep each other company, and when the stress and excitement get to be too much, each acts as the other's reality check. After the ride, they process it start to finish, noting what worked and what could be improved. "I'm getting older and she has more fire than me. I think I'm starting to lose my drive," confesses Valerie.

Valerie has competed in thirty-five U.S. states and in twenty countries. "What makes me happy," she said, "is to take a horse, train it, mold it, and make it successful."

Because of their World Cup championships, the Kanavys (mother and daughter) are recognized internationally and are invited to compete all over the world Valerie enjoys meeting people from many cultures. Having competed in Abu Dhabi and made friends with people from the Arab world has given her a different perspective on the Middle East. "It's like seeing the rest of the world through the local people's eyes," she says. "We're insulated here in the U.S., as far as what's happening in the rest of the world. And until you travel, you don't realize that."

Valerie is especially impressed with the veterinarians from poorer countries, where the technological marvels taken for granted in the United States are generally unavailable. Instead of relying on instruments, they use their hands to diagnose by feel. If the appropriate instrument is available, they use it to confirm what they've already noticed. "We don't have that skill here anymore," says Valerie.

Valerie likes to say that "horses are an accident waiting to happen." What sorts of accidents has she encountered? The worst took place at a competition in 1995. Someone else's horse got loose and took out the Kanavys' electrified fence. Sonny, a horse Danielle had been training for high-level competition, escaped, fell over a cliff, and had to be euthanized.

Out on the trail, less drastic mishaps are not uncommon. Valerie and Danielle had covered seventy-five of the hundred miles in one race when one horse developed muscle soreness and the other tripped, caught his front heel, and ripped it, leaving him lame.

To lose a horse to death or even long-term disability can be devastating. So much care and time goes into training and conditioning a serious endurance competitor. When you compete at high levels, you are working on the edge of both your own and your horse's capability. The possibility for injury and loss is always present. "We're doing a sport," says Valerie philosophically, "and there's got to be setbacks in all sports."

But Valerie is resilient. When she competed in Abu Dhabi, she had barely recovered from a serious staph infection that affected her bones and required treatment with an intravenous antibiotic. The medication sapped her energy, and she'd only finished taking it a week before. But she rallied and did fine. Now, approaching sixty, she still does 50-mile endurance rides with no problem. The 100-milers might tire her out somewhat. In 2008 she raced five 100-mile events in the first 4 months of the year. She placed 25th out of 127 competitors at the Endurance World Championship in Malaysia.

Does Valerie have any questions or misgivings about the way her life has unfolded? She wonders aloud about how her singular focus on endurance competition has affected her as a person. "Your mind has to be churning all the time on how to make it better and what you need to do," she says. "How to play the game better, how to train better. And it tends to make you, not introverted, but it doesn't leave you being a brilliant conversationalist outside of your field." ... I'm not as well-rounded as I should be," she admits. "In some circles, I couldn't carry on a conversation — but I'm not sure that I care to be in those circles."

Her intense focus may have sometimes made her oblivious to other people's needs. Her children, who are now all in their thirties, show no obvious ill effects from their mother's obsession. Danielle, her daughter, shares her passion for horses, so she has probably benefited from it. How about her two sons? Were they shortchanged? When she asked this of Timmy, the youngest, who as a boy was afraid of horses, he told her, "Hey, that's just the way it was. Don't take it personally. It wasn't like you were doing it to me, it's just how it was." Tim works in his father's business, Trevdan Building Supply, lives with his wife and children in the family homestead in Pennsylvania. His older brother Trevon is an insurance salesman and stock broker living in Pennsylvania with his wife and child. It's hard not to beat yourself up for not conforming to the ideal of Supermom, Valerie muses, but she thinks that compared to most of the world's children, hers had it pretty good.

Valerie feels lucky to have been able to make a successful life and career out of something she loves doing. It wasn't something she planned for; it just evolved from her interest in horses, from the natural athleticism that allowed her to ride well even without formal instruction, and from serendipitous meetings along the way with people who influenced her and helped her out. She made good use of the opportunities that came her way. "If something happened to me tomorrow," she says, "I wouldn't feel that I had been short-changed. I'd know that I had a good trip."

Lindy Burch

Cutting Horse Champion

Lindy Competing On Play Peek A Boon

"If you let your deeds speak for yourself and do a good job and don't ask for any special treatment and don't give any special treatment, then pretty soon people respect me for being a cutter, not being a woman who cuts."

In the Bleachers Watching Lindy Compete

We're at the National Cutting Horse Association's futurity (competitions for four-year olds), which attracts cutting's top riders from all over the country. Sixty or more head of cattle roam the arena, bunched together to protect themselves against the unfamiliar sights and sounds. Lindy Burch and her sorrel Bet on Freckles are ready to go. While she is waiting her turn to compete, Lindy checks out the cattle for a good twenty minutes, intensely focused, noting those that seem like good cutting prospects, the ones that are healthy-looking, with good eyes, not wild, but curious — the ones that the cutting pros say "get a-hold of the horse." She notes their markings carefully, so she'll make no mistake about which cows she wants to cut; there may be 30 different cows she's got her eye on. She also makes mental note of which cows have already been "worked" by competitors. A likely cow is intelligent, respectful of the horse but not afraid of it; it's not likely to "throw its tail and run off," as Lindy puts it. Decades of experience have honed her instincts. She is rarely wrong.

Like her fellow competitors on the pro cutting circuit, Lindy is assisted by two herd holders and two turnback people. The herd holders hold the herd at the middle of the back fence, where the cattle congregate. They are told which cows Lindy is looking for. As Lindy focuses on her cow, they'll drive the other cattle out of the way. The turnback people are out in front; they roll the cow back to her, as Lindy describes it, to "give me as much play and challenge from that cow as I can handle — to improve my work and make it as competitive or strong as I can." Once Lindy selects which cow she wants to work, she and her horse quietly walk into the herd and separate the cow from the rest.

The clock starts when the horse has maneuvered the cow about 50 feet in front of the herd. Once the cow is cut, the rider must loosen her reins, called "dropping" the reins, and let the horse do the work. Bet on Freckles knows the drill. The stallion's nose is low to the ground; sometimes he looks like he's dragging his butt. The cow weaves all over and the horse follows the cow's movements with lightning fast speed, all on a loose rein, nose to nose, eyeball to eyeball, accurately mirroring the cow and blocking her every move. One of Lindy's hands is on the horn of the saddle, the other on the reins; she watches intently as the cow moves first one way, then the other, then stops, then moves, desperate to get back to her herd.

Even though Lindy is a long-time veteran of the cutting circuit, she looks serious and focused, never allowing her gaze to wander from the cow in front of her. Once she faces the cow she's separated out from the herd, her horse, one of many that Lindy breeds and trains herself at her Weathersfield, Texas ranch, is adept at following the exact motions of the cow. The whole sequence goes on for only seconds — up to a minute for each cow — until the cow seems to give up by turning away, thereby signaling it has stopped making efforts to return to the herd. Then the rider lifts the reins, giving the horse the message to "quit the cow." The cow is then allowed to return to the herd and the rider begins the selection process of the next cow to cut.

In the allotted 2 ½ minutes Lindy knows she has time to cut up to three cows, no more. Unlike many other competitors, even though she has cut two cows and could well stop at that with a high score, she often challenges herself to cut a third. When she completes the 2 ½ minutes, the buzzer sounds, the crowd leaps to their feet and cheers, and Lindy more often than not adds another win to her already exhaustive list of top placements in the cutting arena.

The Competitive Sport of Cutting

Cutting performances are evaluated by five judges according to established criteria. Each judge comes up with a score between 60 and 80. The high and low scores are thrown out and the middle three averaged to determine the score for each run. The rider is judged on his or her ability to stay with the horse as it maneuvers to control the cow and prevent her from rejoining the herd. The judges evaluate how well horse and rider work the herd, the skill they demonstrate in driving and setting up the cow, and the courage with which they handle challenging situations.

Penalties are accrued under these circumstances: when a horse "quits" or loses a cow; if the rider commits to one cow and then switches to another; when horse and rider fail to separate out a single cow from the herd; if the horse falls to the ground; or if the horse "turns tail" to the cow. Each performance at NCHA-approved events is videotaped; if it turns out that the judges erred in assessing penalties, then the score may be adjusted.

Cutting's equivalent of a perfect "10" is 240. No one has ever managed it. Lindy Burch came closest at the 1998 World Finals in Houston, when she scored 233, the highest tally ever achieved in open competition. Her mount was Bet Yer Blue Boons, the dam of Bet on Me 498.

Bet on Me, Lindy's successful syndicated stallion, and his offspring, have earned about $2,000,000 as a group, two-thirds of Lindy's lifetime earnings from cutting, so Lindy's breeding and training prowess has not only given her satisfaction, but also has made her a wealthy woman. "I think it's a wonderful thing that I'm able to work and earn a living doing something that's my passion," she says. "Not a lot of people get to do that. People wait for Fridays to do their passion on the weekend, but I get to work at my passion every day. I'm lucky to get to spend time with exceptional horses. That's what I would do whether it was my job or not. But to get paid to do it — that is a luxury. I'm very fortunate."

Lindy's Girlhood

Lindy Burch, born Linda Jo Fortin in 1951, grew up on horses in rural southern California, where her family moved from her birthplace in Illinois when she was five. By the time she reached tenth grade, her family had moved several times, from Chino to Oxbow to Van Nuys and back to Chino.

Her earliest memory is of herself as a small girl, riding in front of her dad on long trail rides in Illinois, periodically falling asleep and waking to sip water from the canteen that was hanging from his saddle horn. "That was the most natural place to be," she says.

Her father, Larry Fortin, a machine shop owner, loved horses, especially trail riding and even competed a little in endurance riding. He bought Lindy her first mount, a pony named Candy, when she was five. Later she rode Little Beaver, a paint whom she competed in local gymkhanas that included games that tested the speed and agility of horse and rider and she did a little racing. She was a competitive athletic tomboy. Her maternal grandfather had been an equine veterinarian, and it was her dream to follow in his footsteps, even though he died before she was old enough to know him.

Even as a child, Lindy spent hours riding the trails by herself, all day, every day in the summer. Decades before cell phones, she devised an ingenious method to let her mother know where she was. She trained homing pigeons, placed them in her saddlebags, and periodically sent one home with news of her whereabouts. Her dad built a homing cage next to the kitchen window so that whenever one of the birds arrived, her mother could reach out and extract the message from its leg band.

Jean Fortin, Lindy's mother, was intimidated by horses and must have cringed at some of her daughter's riskier horse activities. As a preteen, when the Fortins were living in Van Nuys, Lindy would ride over to a huge dam right in the middle of the city, sometimes flooded, sometimes not, known for attracting "hobos" or homeless people, but a wonderful place to ride. Despite Jean's discomfort with horses, she sometimes went to watch her daughter compete — and even brought cookies and drinks outdoors to the family ring when Lindy was training horses. Before she was old enough for a driver's license, Lindy got her first real job, galloping racehorses at a local track.

On Sundays, she and her two younger siblings and parents would pile into the car for a family drive. These excursions were created to please Lindy's mother; since she wasn't athletic, she wouldn't join Lindy and her dad on their horses, so Sunday drives were her style of family recreation. Lindy did whatever she could to get out of going along, but she wasn't always successful — and it was on one of these drives that they passed a cutting competition taking place in the picturesque northern California town of Ojai. They stopped to watch. Lindy, then in her mid-teens, was enthralled. She was determined to learn how to cut.

Serendipitously, Bruce Cahill, a cutting-horse trainer from Kansas, moved in across the road from her family. She started spending every hour she could at his barn, before and after school, weekends and summers. He taught her how to handle a horse and cattle in the cutting arena. At Cahill's barn, Lindy got her start as a turnback person. In helping Bruce train his horses, Lindy began to learn how to "read" the cattle, a talent that has made it possible for her to pick the most advantageous cow to cut from a herd.

Even in Lindy's teenage years, a good cutting horse was a hefty investment and she couldn't afford to buy one. But she was given a valuable broodmare in exchange for exercising racehorses at the track, and when someone offered to trade a cutting horse for that mare, Lindy seized the opportunity. She called her new gelding Mr. Nifty. With Bruce Cahill's coaching, Lindy and Mr. Nifty soon became champions in the novice class competitions at the California Cutting Horse Association. The following year she won the open championship.

Cutting, now a major money-making sport, started as a day-in, day-out task on Western ranches, where working cowboys and their horses cut cattle from the herd so they could be branded or sold. Cutting horses have to be quick, agile, and unafraid of the cattle. Not only must they separate cows from the herd, they must prevent the animals from returning to their herd-mates. To help train and condition their horses, cowboys competed informally with each other. Over the years the contests became better organized, locally, regionally, and nationally, and the purses grew accordingly.

Today futurity competitions (open to four-year olds only) sponsored by the National Cutting Horse Association (NCHA) attract an estimated $3 million a year in sponsorships from corporations that cater to horse and cattle ranches. Top riders can take home tens of thousands of dollars in prize money from a single competition. Horses with the potential to win in top competitions don't come cheap: investors can pay between $100,000 and $350,000 for a well-bred horse.

In one of several relocations to accommodate Larry Fortin's work, the family had moved back to Chino, California, when Lindy was sixteen. Larry had purchased a few more horses, which Lindy decided to train as cutters. People began to notice her horses and asked to buy them because they were so well schooled. Though still an adolescent, Lindy was building herself both a reputation and a business in the cutting horse world.

In high school Lindy was a superstar athlete who excelled at everything she tried, especially track. Her sports teacher, Miss Scheffer, was a strong influence on her. "She was an older lady with gray hair," Lindy recalls, who "drove a '55 black T-bird convertible — just the most gorgeous car. She was about four-foot-ten, tanned, looked like a berry or a walnut. She was a professional back then."

Miss Scheffer started a special class for girls who took competitive sports seriously. "You had to try out for it," Lindy says. "But Miss Scheffer was always pushing, pushing, pushing to be the best that you can be, to always work harder. She was a great role model, just because she was always so focused on teaching sports ... That was probably my first experience with seeing somebody that was that revved up about something. Like I was revved up about, and would clearly become even more, with the horses." Miss Scheffer, however, was not a horse enthusiast; she thought Lindy should focus on tennis.

Lindy also excelled in academics — with a little help from her mother. Jean Fortin, a legal secretary while raising her three children, typed Lindy's school papers and corrected her spelling. And that, says Lindy, is why she never learned to spell.

Back in Chino in Lindy's high school years, she worked cattle at the then famous (later infamous) Rex Ellsworth Ranch. Ellsworth's barn was known primarily for its racehorses, especially the fast and gentle colt Swaps, who had won the Kentucky Derby and become an idol for the race-going public. People could come to Ellsworth's one night a week, pay their five bucks, work cattle, and train their horses to cut. Lindy rode as much as she could at Ellsworth's barn, gaining more visibility — and clients — because of the fame of the ranch. Later the Ellsworth operation deteriorated so badly that in 1975 its neighbors reported that horses were being abused and neglected. The SPCA had to step in to try to save dozens of dying mares, including the dam of Swaps. But when Lindy was there Ellsworth's fame was on the rise in the racing world, and to her his ranch seemed "a marvel of efficiency."

Lindy Flirts With Academia

While competing and training cutting horses in summers, Lindy started college at University of California, Riverside, then transferred to UCLA on a track scholarship. She graduated with a major in biology, intending to go to veterinary school. She didn't get into vet school the first year she applied, but, instead, while at UC Riverside, she briefly taught courses like parasitology and mammalian endocrinology and performed research on cancer in mice. After completing her master's degree in endocrinology, she contemplated going for a doctorate; she could have finished the coursework in another year. At the same time, however, she was getting more and more offers to train horses. "The more I did that," she says, "the less I wanted to be in the basement at the biology lab." Lindy had found her calling.

Competing in the Cutting Arena

As she matured in her chosen sport, she quickly made news. In 1979, riding Diamond Mystery, she won the reserve championship in the

National Cutting Horse Association's open futurity. No woman had ever placed so high in NCHA competition — and the next year, at the age of twenty-nine, she went herself one better by taking the open futurity championship on Miss Royal Mahogany. Her score of 225.5 set a record that was not challenged for the next seventeen years. Later, in 1999, she scored 233, a score that has not yet been exceeded.

Since then Lindy has amassed winnings of more than $3 million and prestige in the cutting-horse field that no other woman has achieved. She is so respected that she was elected the first female president of the fifty-five-year-old National Cutting Horse Association in 2001, after serving as president of the Pacific Coast Cutting Association for two years in the 1980s. While president of NCHA, she was instrumental in making changes in the judging policies and credentials that made the sport of cutting more professional.

Sexism? Nah!

Nevertheless, Lindy and her protégée Kathy Daughn are still the only two women out of the hundreds of men who compete successfully in the professional cutting arena. Women are more visible in the non-pro category, but competing at the pro level takes a commitment and sacrifice that Lindy thinks not many women are willing to make.

But Lindy is used to being in the minority as a woman. As a kid, she usually hung out with the boys because they were better at sports than the girls were. The stronger the competition, the greater the incentive to improve her own skills. "In riding, I wanted to be as good as I could be as a cutting-horse rider, and sex had nothing to do with it," she says now. "It was obvious that in many classes I'm the only woman in it and everybody would play that up. If you let your deeds speak for yourself and do a good job and don't ask for any special treatment and don't give any special treatment, then pretty soon people respect me for being a cutter, not being a woman who cuts. I'm just a competitor in the arena and that I happen to be a woman is secondary."

Lindy's Support Team

Lindy is quick to acknowledge, though, that she didn't get to the top all by herself. Starting with Miss Scheffer and Bruce Cahill, she has been lucky in her mentors. At the top of her list is the legendary Buster Welch, winner of four world championships and five NCHA futurities. Welch has been inspiring cutting-horse people for fifty years with his vision and his sense of adventure. A working cowboy as a young man, Welch has become an avid historian of cowboy and ranch life, seeking to preserve its traditions and pass them on to subsequent generations. Not surprisingly, his own children, grandchildren, and great-grandchildren cut.

Buster Welch's "professionalism and his presentation of himself and his horses are undeniably his signature," Lindy says. "That's always been a benchmark for me. I knew of him and copied everything and read everything he said. I probably met him in the mid-seventies. Never really got to work with him very much, but just got a little bit of osmosis. I tried to pattern a lot of things I wanted my horses to do to look like Buster's. Not a mirror image, not the exact thing, but similar."

George Wheeler, "a great old guy," gave the young Lindy a big break in her early years of competition. George, by then an old man, was riding with Lindy's father when he mentioned his cutting horse. As Lindy tells the tale, "He said, 'I have this cutting horse mare, a great mare, and nobody's smart enough to ride her. I need to find a good trainer.' And my dad says, 'My daughter rides cutting horses.' So this George Wheeler calls me up, and he says, 'I have this horse named Hollywood Rita. Would you like to ride her at a show for me?'"

Lindy was thrilled. She tried out Hollywood Rita and knew immediately that she'd be a great cutting horse, better than any she'd ridden before. George hauled the mare over in a "little old truck," watched Lindy work her, and said, "You're a good fit. You just do what I say and you'll win a lot of money." So she went wherever George would let her ride Rita and the pair did well.

In 1973, she was riding Rita at a cutting event in Imperial, California, when they caught the eye of trainer Larry Reeder. Lindy knew all about Reeder from reading *Cutting Horse Chatter*, the official magazine of the National Cutting Horse Association. "I knew all the pictures and all the statistics, verbatim," she says. "I could repeat anything. It was my bible. So I knew who Larry Reeder was, a top ten guy." She was too shy to introduce herself. Then, at a midwinter fair, after she'd had "a really good run" on a famous stud named Cowbar, Reeder approached her. "I'm just stoked about the whole deal," she recalls, "and he comes up to me and he says, 'Nice run you had. It's a really nice horse — what's your name?' He introduced himself and he says, 'I tell you what. I moved to Wasco [California], and if you ever want to come up, I'll help you.' I'm just about to faint. He said, 'I'll help you, because I have never ever seen anybody that wanted this more than me until you.'"

In 1977, when Lindy was still in her twenties, Ed Smith and his wife, Modine, offered Lindy the opportunity to ride Ms. Safari, a step up from Hollywood Rita. Ed was a small man physically, but a giant in the cutting field. "He was such a great observer, and he could watch somebody do something and make some thoughtful suggestions and make them better, not just me, but anybody working a horse. I just probably soaked it up a little more than most."

He recognized her talents – her timing and balance on a horse, even though he noticed she was not always the most diplomatic person when she felt strongly about something or someone. But his feedback always improved her cutting technique. He encouraged her to "drive out," meaning, Lindy explains, "to drive your cow away from the herd more, so you'd get into a better position. It's all about control of the cow, and it's easier to control the cow if you're far out than if you're right against the herd."

Ed Smith died in 1979. Diamond Mystery, the horse that Lindy rode to the NCHA open futurity reserve championship later that year, was one of his horses. To this day she regrets that Ed was not able to see her win. Modine, Ed's widow, remains one of her closest friends.

While giving a private cutting clinic in Oregon, Lindy met Dan Lufkin, co-founder of the Wall Street firm, Donaldson, Lufkin and Jenrette —and an avid cutting-horse breeder and enthusiast. She later formed a partnership with Lufkin, which culminated in her operating the OxBow Ranch in Carmel, California, in the late 1980s and later the OxBow South in Texas.

Lindy's Ranch

Now Lindy Burch owns the OxBow Ranch, which she used to call The 80 Ranch, a state-of-the-art 160-acre facility near Weatherford, Texas, southwest of Fort Worth. This part of Texas is flat and dry. The roads stretch for miles ahead with nothing on the horizon but more road and more scrubby sagebrush. It's not an area where you can find a restaurant or motel, only ranches and more ranches.

Here she breeds and trains cutting horses and competes successfully at the highest levels of the cutting-horse world. At any given time there are about sixty horses in residence, including the broodmares, weanlings, and yearlings. Three-quarters of them belong to Lindy; the remainder she syndicates (enlists investors to contribute so that she can afford to keep them), like the champion Bet on Me 498, or she boards or trains for other people. She designed the operation herself; it features a barn with more than two dozen roomy stalls, a covered cutting arena, an outdoor roping area, and a spacious office attached to the barn. The whole facility is exceptionally clean and well-organized, expressing Lindy's insistence upon a high standard of care for her horses.

Lindy says her horses are like "Fabergé eggs," priceless and fragile. Unlike Fabergé eggs, however, they don't just sit quietly on a shelf. They are constantly moving and traveling and being exposed to the possibility of injury and illness. Not surprisingly, their care is as state-of-the-art as the facility. Lindy demands perfection from herself and doesn't let her employees lapse either. When I visited the ranch, it was March, when shades of dusty brown dominated the landscape; the horses were fit, beautifully turned out, and friendly.

Although Lindy decided against going to veterinary school, her university studies aren't going to waste. "I have a lot of knowledge in veterinary medicine and I do all of the herd health maintenance here," she says. "I think it's really helped my horse training to know what I know about

Lindy's Weatherford Ranch

veterinary medicine and physiology from school and from teaching for two years. I wouldn't trade what I've done to be a vet. In my position I get to dabble in medicine, marketing, and public relations with the syndication of my stallion, Bet on Me 498. I get to dabble in politics by being president of the National Cutting Horse Association. And I do clinics in Brazil, Australia, Italy. I get to go all over the world with cutting."

A Day in the Life of Lindy

Lindy gets up early in the morning; in the summer, when it is too hot to train during the day, she must be outside working before the sun comes up. She goes to bed early to maintain that schedule. It's not a life that can easily accommodate a live-in relationship. In 1974, the year she got her master's degree, she married Frank Burch, a non-pro cutter. They eventually divorced. Later she had another long-term relationship that also came to an end. "It has to be my way," she says. "There's no discussion whether I'm going to work horses before the sun comes up or we're going on a trip or we're going to the theater tonight. It's something I have to do. It's my job. To be where I am, it's had to be pretty much full-court press." As a woman, she can't count on the support that some of her male colleagues take for granted. "In order to be competitive with all the guys, I have to work like they do," she notes. "I don't have a wife that's going to cook and take care of the kids and the house and go to the cleaners while I'm riding. I have somebody who works for me do that. It's not an obstacle to me, but it's my choice, a way of life."

Although Lindy has not had children of her own, she is a surrogate mom for many young people who have come to train with her. "I have a lot of kids, but I don't have them. I don't miss having a child of my own when I have several," she says. "I'm like their stepmom." She donates clinics to the youth of her community. Some of her former students have become lifelong friends, as well as her competition in the cutting arena. It's especially rewarding when a young person she took on as a novice grows into a successful competitor.

What does Lindy do for R&R, when she's not working or competing? On Sundays, she rides around her ranch for pleasure. Maybe she'll pony another horse to give it exercise. Sometimes she takes horses in training out on her own and others' ranches to help gather cattle and cut just for fun.

Colt On Lindy's Ranch

When her schedule permits, she may take a horse or two with her to visit a friend in Colorado and ride all over the beautiful country around Crested Butte. She rides her cutting horses, because they are the best broke and the smartest. "I don't like dumb horses any more than I like dumb people," she says.

She muses about what she'll do after she gives up competing. She's not at a loss for things she loves. She'll always be involved with horses in some way. She loves to hunt birds, thinks she might take up golf, and relishes the outdoor life.

Many of Lindy's longtime friends and associates are in the cutting industry. When they're not competing, they might shoot birds or rock-climb or ride horses for pleasure. Her best friend is not a cutting professional, but she does cut, so she knows what it is about for Lindy. She owns a restaurant in California. Lindy has a completely different talent that she expressed in helping her friend design her house and barn.

She designed her own home at her Weatherford ranch, a comfortable 2500 square feet rock and timber house. It has comfortable porches all around, to shade from the hot Texas sun. Inside it has rough-hewn beams, a high ceiling with a loft, and it is filled with equine sculptures, paintings and Western memorabilia.

Although intense and perfectionistic in her horsemanship and truthful to the point where she can inadvertently insult someone, she has another side; her friends comment about her ability to mimic singers, be silly, and entertain with her musicianship. That's not a quality she often lets the public see.

At age 58, Lindy is still competing at the highest levels of her field. She still gets a rush from competing. She loves the pressure. She likes "putting a run together that will be one of the most competitive runs." Barring serious injury, she thinks she could stay there another five years. "When it's your time, it's your time," she says philosophically. "I've been very lucky. I have a plate on my fibula from an injury incurred during a racquetball match. A guy fell on me. Broke my fibula. I've broken a couple of ribs, where a horse has fallen on me, and I have bad knees from everything from powder-puff football to riding to snow skiing."

How long does she keep competing? "Until I'm not at the top," she replies.

Julie Krone

Winning Jockey

"I was overflowing with drive and determination and nothing was going to get in the way of my success."

Julie Krone was barely five years old when the first women jockeys in the United States started getting their licenses. When she entered the race-riding world at the age of seventeen, in 1981, women were still an anomaly, particularly in high-stakes races. Most trainers and owners were loath to put women on their horses. On those rare occasions when Julie did get the opportunity to race, male jockeys sometimes tried to run her mount off the track. By being alternately brash and charming, Julie convinced a few trainers to try her. Once they did, they recognized her intuitive feel for her horses and her steely determination to win. She would crouch above that little saddle, barely 100 pounds, 4 feet 10 inches tall, and guide those big horses to the finish line with the subtlest flutter of the reins, the fewest cracks of the whip. She seemed to know how to settle each horse, to keep him calm with her body and voice. No one else rode like that.

But ability alone couldn't vanquish the prejudice against women who dared to guide these 1,200-pound creatures around a track at nearly forty miles an hour, with barely enough space between riders to wedge a thumb. This tiny girl with her high squeaky voice and a ten-year-old's figure had to seduce each owner, each trainer, into trying her out—seduce not with sex, but with Dunkin Donuts brought to the barn and a killer handshake offered to show these men that she had the grit it took to race ride.

During her early years in this macho, often hostile world, Julie tried to be one of the guys, and a tougher guy than any of those who were trying to hurt her. She would blow her nose on the ground by holding one nostril; or slug another jockey who tried to sabotage or endanger her on the track. She became what's called a "diabolical rider"—one who didn't hesitate to pin other riders in place so they couldn't move, then break through and win by a nose. No one guessed that for her it was a life-or-death matter, that she felt like a nothing—unless she won.

One drawback to being a pioneer is having neither road maps nor mentors to guide your steps or to give you a heads-up when you're heading in the wrong direction. Wanting to be noticed for the expert rider she was, desperate to convince trainers and owners to put her on their horses, Julie often alienated those she wanted to impress. Her belligerence got her into trouble with fellow jocks, with grooms, and, ultimately, with herself. More than once track officials suspended her for her quarrelsome behavior.

Julie's Unusual Childhood

Julie's prodigious talent and determination as well as her shortcomings can be traced back to her upbringing. Judi Krone, Julie's mother, was passionate about riding from a young age, but she grew up in a Chicago neighborhood and a strict religious environment; she had to sneak around to hide her interest from her parents. She wasn't able to start riding until she was in high school, though she had always dreamed of becoming a horsewoman. Once Judi's family moved to the suburbs, she found ways around her parents' obstinate prejudice against horseback riding. Excellence came quickly, thanks to her intuitive way of communicating with horses—a skill that Julie must have absorbed by osmosis. Despite her late start and lack of family support, Julie's mom even became a Michigan state equestrian champion.

Judi was determined to give her daughter the freedom she had not had as a youngster. Once, when Julie was two years old and still in diapers, Judi lifted her onto the saddle to show a prospective buyer that a horse was gentle enough for children. The horse cantered off to the rail and Julie grabbed the reins, turned him around, and casually trotted back. She has been passionate—and fearless—around horses ever since.

Judi and her husband, Don, a photographer and junior high art teacher, provided little structure and few limits for their two children, Julie and her older brother, Donnie. In her 1995 memoir, *Riding for My Life*, Julie wrote that her mother wanted to make a life for them that was "filled with animals, friends, and country fun. There were no fences to keep us in, no locked doors, rules, or set mealtimes. I was as wild as the animals on the farm, and just as free." At the age of six, she was allowed to go off trail-riding on her own. At thirteen, she donned a loincloth, stood atop her bareback horse, and galloped at full speed toward the barn, only straddling the horse's back at the last moment to avoid being decapitated by the barn door. This was Julie; both of her parents reveled in their daughter's guts to pull off stunts like that. Instead of screeching "Be careful," her dad asked her to repeat the trick so he could photograph her.

The upside was that Julie had no qualms about handling a Thoroughbred racehorse running at top speed on a high-stakes track. The downside was that she had no clue how to behave in a professional racing environment, nor in her personal life.

Judi Krone was Julie's first, and practically her only riding instructor, with the exception of the renowned dressage trainer Chuck Grant, whom Judi brought to Michigan in 1979. Grant was instrumental in persuading Judi to take her teenage daughter's jockey dream seriously. After he watched Julie cantering around the arena while standing on the back of her Arabian stallion, Ralphy, he was convinced.

Judi taught Julie everything she knew, based on her own knowledge of dressage and her intuitive feel for horses. Judi's students loved her, but her daughter was often anxious in her presence because Judi could be so demanding and unpredictable. One day Judi might gently caress her daughter's hair while they drove home from a horse show, but the next day Judi might throw stones at Julie for not measuring up to her expectations.

Being a quick study, Julie didn't get too many stones thrown at her. Later her mother recalled that from babyhood Julie knew she could do anything physical. At nine or ten Julie watched another kid ride a bike with no hands. After a couple of minutes' practice, she was doing it herself. With horses, she was equally self-assured. "I'd see someone do things in a systematic way and once I learned the system, I could just copy it," Julie remembers. "Even if I didn't have an understanding of it. I'd see somebody do something with a horse, and I only needed one time, especially if they were really good. And my mom was really good."

Julie was so agile and coordinated that at one point she thought of joining the circus as an acrobat. She never did, but she frequently demonstrated her acrobatic abilities on horseback, with her parents' encouragement and with the neighbors looking on in dismay. Her passion for horses precluded virtually all other interests. As a youngster, she traveled all over Michigan with her mom to compete in horse shows and came back with ribbons for dressage, jumping, and trail riding.

Julie's father, Don Krone, was as passionate in his way as his wife was in hers, but his interests were more solitary. He had "a terrible social disorder," as Julie puts it: he could, and still can, stay home, reading, doing his art, photography, or using the computer, and never miss being with people. Chit-chat socializing made him uncomfortable—it isn't Julie's forte either—and he was withdrawn to the point of being reclusive. He also could get hyper-involved in whatever he was passionate about. In Julie's memoir, she describes his tendency to disappear into his darkroom for hours at a time, unaware of time passing. She also absorbed some of his artistic inclinations; as a child, the only classes she loved were art and gym.

Julie's first horse was a naughty and mean pony she called Filly. She credits Filly with teaching her to ride well, "Everything I did with Filly was an experiment," she wrote in her memoir. "But by experimenting I learned to ride instinctively. There are some things a rider has to learn by touch, by reaction—lessons no instructor can give. When I rode her, she would constantly plot ways to buck me off.... Once I had mastered Filly's stubborn nature, she performed and reacted ten times better than other ponies."

Julie was a tiny girl who did not mature at the time her classmates did. She always felt socially insecure, unsure of how to behave in groups. She struggled with schoolwork and never thought she was smart. Years later, when she was thirty, Julie finally discovered she had learning disabilities and ADHD (attention deficit hyperactivity disorder). People with ADHD have poor concentration, are distractible, do impulsive things like race toward the barn door standing on top of their horse, and are hyperactive in mind and body. As they grow older, they usually get a bit more mellow physically and find ways to compensate, but school is a disaster for these kids. In the 1970s, when Julie was in school, the disorder was not well understood, and children with ADHD didn't receive the help they needed. Many became convinced that they were stupid or lazy.

To add to her woes, when she was fourteen, Julie's parents divorced, with hard feelings on both sides. Relations between her parents were so tense that Julie didn't dare mention one to the other. She felt pulled apart by the two of them; in her memoir, she remembers her parents dividing their belongings, including her bedroom furniture. "Are they going to split me in half too?" she wailed to herself. She saw her dad only on weekends. Earlier, she had tried marijuana with her best friend; now she started using it to comfort herself. She had a few bouts with depression at this time, a harbinger of things to come.

Looking back, Julie thinks that her parents' divorce crystallized her determination to become a jockey. It was an example of a coping style she later perfected: "selective amnesia," she calls it. Rather than give in to despair about her broken family, she focused all her fantasies and energy on getting herself ready to become the jockey she wanted to be. She and her mother became inseparable buddies, bonded by their love for horses, but their relationship was not easy. She conveyed the contradictions in a poem she wrote for her English teacher, Miss Shilling:

(with permission from her memoir *Riding For My Life*)

Mother, you say that I'm a sneaky
kid and that maybe you should
have when I was a baby
drowned me in a lake
you've never baked me a cake.
Then why do I love you
like I do—this I wondered
as I grew.
Your [sic] the one who bought
my first horse. You taught me
how to ride and be the best
(of course).
I know that you love me dearly
You tell me more than once yearly.
I can't be perfect for I'm
Only seventeen you see but then
If I was whose fault would it be?

The Start of Race Track Life – Early Glory and Early Misery

Julie's racetrack life started the summer she was fifteen; her mother altered her birth certificate to make it look like she was already sixteen, the minimum age to get a job at the track. The night before they set out on the six-hour trip from Eau Claire, Michigan, to Churchill Downs, in Kentucky, her mom came home late from her job at a bar. Julie was too excited to sleep; she waited up for her mother. At 1:30 in the morning, Judi and Julie went out for a ride on their horses, singing "Don't Fence Me In" at the top of their lungs.

Judi stuck around at Churchill Downs just long enough to know that her young daughter had found a job and place to live. Julie landed a job as a "hotwalker," walking and hosing down the horses after exercise until their temperature and pulse come down to normal. She worked for Clarence and

Donna Picou, a couple who turned out to be the first racetrack family who took her in and befriended her. Clarence noticed how comfortable Julie was around horses; three weeks after her arrival, he promoted her to groom. It wasn't long before he allowed her to gallop horses down the stretch at Churchill Downs.

Against all bets, just two years later, in February 1981, Julie "broke her maiden"—won her first race as an apprentice jockey—on Lord Farkle at Tampa Bay Downs. She was not quite eighteen years old. To commemorate this event, her fellow jockeys accosted her in the locker room and covered her with a concoction of peanut butter, black shoe polish, baby powder, and shaving cream, the traditional hazing for every new jockey who wins a first race.

In the early years when Julie was trying to support herself on the track, she sometimes lacked money for gas or food, but she was enterprising about taking care of herself. She apprenticed with several trainers, some of whom became like family for her while she was on the road. As a young adult, she had a lot to learn about how to treat others and herself. She credits some of these surrogate families with taking her under their wing and giving her valuable advice and support.

Perhaps most important among the families she adopted was Chick Lang, who was her agent for a time, his wife, Jean, and their four children. Julie admired Jean immensely and wanted to be the kind of person she was. The Langs were Julie's idea of a real family, one with expectations about behavior that were foreign to Julie. Once, early in her stay with the Lang family, she was late for dinner. The Langs waited, plates heaped with food that they didn't touch until she appeared. She was flabbergasted. The Krone family probably never sat down to a meal together. Often there was no food in the house, not for lack of money but for lack of organization and interest in mundane matters. Julie and her brother were known to resort to dog food in an emergency. Later, after Julie took some wrong turns in her life and was suspended from the track for using drugs, her big regret was letting Jean Lang down.

For many years Julie floundered, yearning for attention and love, but not knowing how to have an intimate relationship or even a friend. Back in high school, she had been dismissed by boys as a runt or a tomboy, so her experience with romantic relationships was minimal. And her parents' relationship taught her little about what it means to share interests, communicate, and be consistent. Then at the age of eighteen, in 1981, she met Steve Brown, an assistant to John Forbes, a well-known trainer. Steve recognized her talent and put her on some of Forbes's horses, hiding from his boss the fact that Julie was a girl. After they had known each other a year, to Julie's amazement Steve asked her out on a date. She loved the idea of having a boyfriend and enjoyed being with his family. This was a first for her.

When Julie finally met John Forbes himself, she was honored that he invited her to ride his horses, a boost for her career because of his reputable owners and exceptional horses. But it also posed a dilemma, one that the romantically inexperienced Julie had had little occasion to confront before. Forbes explained that his clients had to be assured that she was riding their horses because of her ability, not because of her relationship with Steve. He made it plain that their liaison wasn't good for business, his or hers. Forbes put the question to her bluntly: Do you love Steve enough to give up riding my horses? She decided that she didn't. Forbes cared about her career as a jockey; he worked hard to get other trainers and owners to give her rides. Coincidentally (or maybe not) Steve broke up with her. Even though Julie had chosen to ride Forbes's horses rather than maintain her relationship, still Steve was her first love and she was devastated by the rejection. She began to have thoughts of suicide and catapulted into a losing streak on the track. This was one of several serious depressions in the young Julie's life.

Another came when the impressionable Julie was briefly drawn into using cocaine, barely knowing what the drug was. Plenty of her racetrack heroes used it, so how bad could it be? In 1982, while working at Pimlico Racetrack in Maryland, she was busted for having marijuana in her car. She had to attend a drug abuse program and pee in a jar regularly, and, worst of all, she was barred from racing for sixty days. She had never been away from horses for that long. That convinced her that using illegal drugs wasn't worth jeopardizing her career, her whole world, for. Drugs had also prompted her estrangement from her mother the year before; Judi had told her, "Don't bother to call until you clean up your act."

In 1986, when Julie was twenty-three, Judi Krone was diagnosed with cancer. Julie had just begun to live out the dream they shared for her, to race horses. When she asked her mother what she could do for her, Judi Krone said, "Win." And win she did. Sometimes Julie won several races in a single day, and she'd call Judi in her rehab hospital to report each win. Judi beat the odds and lived until 1999 — long enough to see her daughter becoming the famous jockey she had aspired to be. By 1988, Julie had become the female jockey to have won the most races: 1,205! Judi could take pride in some of Julie's firsts: she became the first woman to race-ride in Tokyo, when she represented the United States in the 1990 Japan Cup, one of the richest races in the world, attracting an international field of competitors. The riders were treated like royalty, and as many as 170,000 came to watch. Her dad accompanied her to Tokyo and shared her incredulity when she met her childhood hero, jockey Steve Cauthen. Her dad was even more thrilled to watch her beat him in a race. And in 1993, Julie's mom watched Julie win the Belmont Stakes on Colonial Affair and enter the record books as the first woman to win a Triple Crown race.

Julie and her mother had a tumultuous relationship, but the bond between them endured. Julie says she is still learning from her mother, years after her death. Judi Krone "never perceived just the bad or just the good and could see both sides of an issue," Julie says now. She can do that too and credits her mother for her ability. Likewise she absorbed some of her mother's tremendous faith that "if you follow your heart, the rest will follow."

Racing At Monmouth Park, NJ in the 1980s

Julie Makes History as Top Jockey

In 1989, Julie appeared on the cover of *Sports Illustrated*. She had arrived! David Letterman, Jay Leno, and Johnny Carson welcomed her to their shows. By this time, she was more comfortable in her own skin and could speak her mind with more ease. Later, after she moved to California in 1999, Julie became a television commentator herself. She has worked for TVG racing network and the Hollywood Park simulcast network, as well as doing commentary for other special shows, like the 2000 Breeders' Cup at Churchill Downs, a race she had been the first woman to compete in just a few years before.

As Julie wrote in *Riding for My Life*, "Sooner or later every jockey falls from her horse." She's incurred a few injuries over the years, some more serious than others. At Saratoga in 1993 she suffered a fall that nearly killed her. The long recuperation demanded as much courage and perseverance as her racing career. The fiercely independent Julie could no longer take care of herself. In learning to depend upon others, she finally realized how many people loved and cared about her as a person, not just as a star. In her first press conference in the hospital, she cried, overwhelmed by her feelings about what had happened and by her own vulnerability. This was new. She had always kept a stiff upper lip with the media, never daring to show much of her true self.

When she returned to the track after her recovery, she was terrified that she would fall again and — perhaps even worse — that she might have lost her touch with horses. She soon won another race at Belmont, however, on Consider the Lily, a horse she had known and loved as a two-year-old filly. She wrote in her memoir: "I was back, but I finally understood I had never been gone. And that the something inside me that always fought to win and never gave in to the pain and that accepted no less than one-hundred-ten percent, had never been gone either, because that something was simply me."

In 1995, Julie married a man she had known at the track at Saratoga. The marriage lasted only four years and she took the breakup very hard. She had had a difficult time as a teenager when her parents split up, and now her own divorce triggered some of the same feelings.

The following year, 1996, overwhelmed by her success and all the attention she received as an outstanding woman in an almost exclusively male sport, Julie hit a rocky stretch of road. A fall "fried" her, threw her into a two-month-long tailspin during which she completely lost confidence on the track and started losing badly. Previously a confident, relaxed person on a horse, one who never allowed herself to remember bad things like previous falls, now she could not get dire possibilities out of her mind. She was beset by anxieties and fears of getting killed. Even small everyday occurrences could prompt a panic attack. She contemplated ways to kill herself. She had toyed with suicidal ideas back when her first boyfriend, Steve, had broken up with her, but quickly talked herself out of it. This was more serious.

"I couldn't talk, she told *New York Times* journalist Robert Lipsyte in May 2000. "The straw didn't break the camel's back; it gutted the sucker, left the camel for dead. I was numb, couldn't think. I was afraid of horses, hated riding."

She felt as if she had missed the class where they taught people how to handle traumas, as if, she recalled, "I had to do this really hard test. I never got to study and I didn't know these things. I didn't get it. I thought, 'Did they talk about this? I don't remember this.' That's what it felt like ... It couldn't have gotten any worse, from divorce, to mental illness, to physical illness, death in the family, cross-country move. I'm talking, just put your head down on the pillow at night and there was no relief from any direction you looked. And it was brutal."

The "down" period went on for five or six years, during which her mother died and Julie moved to California. Fortunately, Julie consulted a psychiatrist, Tom Qualtere, a horse owner and Saratoga track enthusiast; he told her she had PTSD, post-traumatic stress disorder. With therapy and later antidepressant medication, she slowly found her way back to herself, but this time to an adult person with many more coping skills and more self-esteem than the younger Julie had possessed. She told reporter Lipsyte that in therapy "I felt full and empty at the same time, joyful and like I was peeling off my skin."

Even though Julie had come a long way in feeling confident and comfortable about her success, she found dealing with the media especially difficult when she was depressed. "I just sat there and I couldn't even talk to myself, I was so frozen," she recalls. "I didn't know how to sort it out or where to start. I let everything gang up on me at once. There were these people standing there that wanted to talk to me [and] I couldn't even form sentences. I used to say, 'I can't talk right now.' When I did go out, I didn't have anything to say. I just said, 'He ran really good and I don't know what happened.' They said, 'We waited twenty minutes for that?' That just struck me. They just want to hear something."

She emerged from this tumultuous period with more clarity and more self-assurance. She still retains a protective shield with people, though; she's more comfortable with strangers than with people she knows somewhat. She doesn't like it when people assume they know her because they've read about her or seen her on TV. And she's always more comfortable with kids, whom she sees as honest about wanting to hang out with her for her own qualities, not because she's famous.

Julie temporarily retired in 1999 when her mother's cancer, long in remission, returned in full force. Judi Krone died later that year. Three and a half years later Julie returned and started winning races again. By then she was married for the second time, to award-winning sportswriter Jay Hovdey. By now, she knew what love was about and was not inclined to put her riding career above her family. She also had started doing sports commentating on television. So, she began to have a life outside of the track. Then in 2003, at Santa Anita Park, she took a bad fall and landed in the hospital with three compressed vertebrae and fractured bones in her lower back, as well as ligament and muscle damage.

On her first day back in the saddle after that injury, a jockey she'd ridden with for years was killed in a race. Just two months earlier, the great jockey Laffit Pincay had broken his neck in a fall. He survived, but the injury forced him to stop riding. Finally it sunk in just how dangerous race-riding can be. And now she had something besides race-riding to live for. In 2004, she retired once again. She ended her career with 3,704 wins and more than $90 million in purse earnings. And a normal family life to return to.

Julie Treasures Her Normal Life as Wife and Mom

Julie lives in Southern California now with her husband, Jay. He writes for the *Daily Racing Form* and *Reader's Digest* and has published three books. "He's very good," she says. "He's E. B. White good, just fun to read. He loves horse racing and the people in it. Sometimes he writes something and he'll tell me a story about it and he says, 'Can't make this stuff up!' Like 'Three-legged Horse Wins Derby.' No way."

Julie and Jay talked about adopting a child; it's something she had thought about for a long time, even when she was single. Then, to her surprise, Julie found herself pregnant. She gave birth to Lorelei Judith Hovdey in September of 2005. "Motherhood has been the primary new activity in my life," Julie says, "and I devote a lot of time to making sure Lorelei is growing up healthy and strong. I have some firm, thoroughly researched opinions about what should and should not go into that precious little body. We have been rewarded with a little girl who is already connecting to her world in wonderful ways. She is a real chatterbox who is passionate about her dancing, her costumes, her mom and dad, and her pony, Miss Piggy, a palomino that she is already riding all by herself with careful attendants, of course. She is so brave and daring, I am anxious for her to grow up a little more physically so she can be everything she's dreaming she can be."

After being intensely involved with horses and racing for two decades, Julie is striking out in new directions. When I met her for the first time, in October 2004, she was learning to surf. It took her three years to feel confident about getting up on a surfboard. "And I'm just now getting it right," she said with satisfaction, and perhaps some relief. "I would go out for a surf session and just never get on the back of my surfboard. Just paddle and get knocked off my board, paddle and get knocked off... I'd do that for an hour. And that's all I could accomplish in a day."

Then, after paddling and falling over and over again, she'd catch a wave just right. It would seem so perfect, so easy. "And then everything goes wrong for about three days and you get wiped out a lot, you fall off a lot," she says. "That one time keeps dragging you back in."

Music, another interest, offers similar challenges and rewards. Julie was taking ukulele lessons when I met her. "Music is scary because you have to be so brave," she says. "It's dangerous. It's so expressive. Especially if you sing. You get some chords down, and you think, I got this now. And you think you're being cool and you mess it up."

Julie has also begun a career as an inspirational public speaker, attracted to the idea of conveying to her audiences what she has learned as a woman who grew up with some obstacles, but with the determination to succeed at something she was passionate about. With her experience as a TV sports personality, her vivacious nature, and her strong opinions, she is bound to be a natural in this competitive arena, much as she was on the track.

As an adult, Julie had long been one to want to learn and stretch herself. Even though she dropped out of high school as a youngster, Julie eventually had earned a diploma at age 33 in 1996—right around the time the Russian hockey team misbehaved in the Olympics. *The New York Daily News* called her up to say that in their "Winners and Losers" column the loser was the Russian hockey team and the winner Julie Krone for going back to school and getting her diploma. She's proud of the accomplishment — and she's continued her education both on her own and by taking courses at a local college.

Julie Telling Her Story To Karma

Purely by chance, she discovered the discipline of Parelli Natural Horsemanship, a method of communicating with horses that, in the words of the Parelli website, allows "horse lovers at all levels and disciplines to achieve success without force, partnership without dominance, teamwork without fear, willingness without intimidation, and harmony without coercion." Julie waxes enthusiastic about learning the Parelli method, feeling it brought her back to horses. She hopes that she can be instrumental in introducing it on the racetrack, where horses can get so wound up at the starting gate that they are either frozen in fear or out of control. She believes that the reason she stayed alive on thousands of horses in her twenty-two-year race-riding career was because of her intuitive ability to read the horse and communicate subtly. The Parelli philosophy coincides well with the one her mother taught her, she notes: "In the world of Parelli, horses are our partners in fun and games. There are no commands, only requests. We ask permission of our horse to enter their circle and participate in their world."

Kathy Kusner

Olympic Jumper & Pioneering Jockey

Kathy Competing On Untouchable, Wiesbaden, Germany

"You only live once that we know of. If you want to do some other things, you've got to un-nail yourself from the floor. So, I'm un-nailed and, consequently, I've had many new chapters, many interesting things that weren't just repeating."

The *Chronicle of the Horse* picked Kathy Kusner as one of the fifty most influential horsemen of the twentieth century, and it's no wonder. She was only nineteen when she was asked to train with the U.S. Equestrian Team (USET) — one of the first two women to be so honored. She represented the United States in three Olympic Games, Tokyo in 1964, Mexico City in 1968, and Munich in 1972, where she won a silver medal. While competing at the highest levels of show jumping, Kathy also rode races, both on the flat and over hurdles. She was the first woman to ride in the Maryland Hunt Cup, widely considered the most difficult timber racecourse in the world. Snowden Carter, former editor of *Maryland Horse Magazine*, said of the Hunt Cup, "It's tough and demanding. Anybody not up to do it is going to get killed. It's strictly big league stuff." And, if that's not enough, Kathy became the first woman in the United States to procure a jockey's license, winning the right for women to participate fully in the "sport of kings."

To this day Kathy Kusner follows her curiosity and passions. She's not one to shy away from a challenge. In her sixties when I met her, Kathy was fit, silver-haired, and pretty. She volunteered to give me a ride to meet her friend and fellow horsewoman Julie Krone; our interview took place as we drove south from Los Angeles toward San Diego. Kathy was uneasy talking of personal matters, but enthusiastic about the things she cares about. Although the horse world has been a cornerstone of her life for decades, it is not her only passion. She shared many of those interests with me, ensconced in her little Toyota, "the cheapest car I could find," while she expertly navigated the freeways of Southern California.

Kathy's Independent Childhood

Kathy's family had no interest in horses whatsoever, so her first big challenge was finding a way to get involved herself. She begged and pleaded and finally her parents bought her a pony named Champ. Her father built Champ a shed and a paddock. Eventually he even rebuilt a trailer so Kathy could get her pony to lessons and shows. But the deal was that Kathy had to earn money to support Champ's maintenance.

She pressed Champ into service; they gave pony rides to earn his keep. Kathy pretty much taught herself to ride — she didn't have tack and so rode bareback. Then at a horse show she saw riders jumping with saddles and using what "looked like a million reins" — probably the bridles had

Pelham bits, which require two reins; maybe they were using martingales or breastplates as well. She was fascinated. She had to meet the trainer of those kids!

Not only did she manage to introduce herself, she prevailed upon the teacher, Jane Marshall Dillon, to give her lessons in exchange for stable work. Mrs. Dillon (as she was called back in the 50s), a disciple of Captain Vladimir Littauer who was a master of forward-seat riding, had established the Junior Equitation School to teach the best young riders in the area. It was fortuitous that Kathy discovered Mrs. Dillon, a real equitation professional and author of *School for Young Riders*, a classic that is still being read today. Kathy rode the school horses and worked in the barn. As she gained skill as a rider, she showed schooling horses; later she was asked to ride other people's higher level horses. Soon she was winning her share of ribbons on some of the best show hunters and jumpers in the area.

Kathy's family was totally uninvolved in her equestrian activities. They did not even know where she was competing or when she won. From a young age Kathy was an independent person, as were her parents. "They had their own lives and interests," Kathy explains. "They weren't dependent upon being entertained by something that I was doing. My mother taught school and swimming and was a big nature person and went on trips with the Audubon Society. She didn't need to be bored at a horse show. My father was a scientific person. He made several telescopes. Also taught calculus at night. He was a mathematician. They were doing what they liked. It was great. No one was being dragged anywhere." She sees this as a gift; her parents gave her tacit permission to conduct her life the way she wished to and were pleased she was doing something she was passionate about.

Education was important to both of Kathy's parents. Her father put himself through college and graduate school by driving a taxicab; he eventually earned a doctorate. Kathy was a poor student. She got Ds and worse; she failed courses and had to take them over in summer school — where she sometimes failed again. Public school in Virginia in the 1950s, as she recalls it, was "worse than jail." The racial segregation, not only at school but in the community, disturbed her, even at a young age. The rules were rigid — girls had to wear skirts to school! — and the lessons uninspiring to a young girl who much preferred to be at the barn learning to shoe a horse and developing other useful skills.

Kathy missed high school graduation because she was out of town at a horse show. Her mother had to pick up her diploma. As Kathy tells the story, the principal told her mother, "Mrs. Kusner, your daughter doesn't deserve this, but you do." Kathy feared her mother would be angry with her for missing this important event, but instead, when she got home, her mother was holding her diploma, "laughing hysterically, like she'd gone crazy. She was just relieved that I'd gotten a diploma."

As an adult, Kathy started taking and enjoying courses at local community colleges. She loves the diversity she's found there, so different from what she experienced in the segregated Virginia of her childhood. She's become an inveterate learner, soaking up new things, digging deeply into whatever intrigues her. When she is satisfied with one subject, she proceeds to the next. She regrets that her parents didn't live long enough to appreciate her passion for learning. Her mother, an avid birdwatcher, might be surprised to know that Kathy loves going birding with the Audubon Society; as a girl, she considered this pursuit worse than "eating ground glass."

By the time she reached her late teens, Kathy was competing in every horse show she could get to, riding some of the best horses in the country. She'd ride any horse anyone offered to her and thrived on every horse-related challenge. Theodora Ayer Randolph, General George S. Patton's niece, bred and raised her own hunters and was known during her lifetime as the "first lady of fox hunting"; Randolph asked Kathy to ride her horses. She also rode in local timber races and point-to-points — unrecognized races over rigid timber fences. This was the only racing a girl could do in those days, and it was pretty rough-and-tumble; anything was tolerated, including a lot of drinking. Being female was no handicap in the bush league races. "A space alien could have ridden," she says now.

Getting to Be Known in Prestigious Places And Making It to the USET

Since she was adept at "catch riding" — riding unfamiliar horses — top owners and trainers asked her to ride for them. And she won with both racehorses and show horses, all the way up to Madison Square Garden. Everyone in the world of competitive riding knew her name. "I got to the point where I could do what they wanted, which was to showcase their horses," she says. "And if the rider is doing a decent job, that's also showcasing the rider. It was a perfect situation for me." Champ was both the first and the last horse she ever owned. "I didn't have the money or the need," she explains. "This way I had a lot more flexibility to ride all different horses and not be restricted from new possibilities because you own something. Which has been my philosophy in life, to own as little as possible."

Kathy first saw the United States Equestrian Team (USET) at a horse show in Harrisburg, Pennsylvania, where she was grooming for Jane Marshall Dillon. She was immediately struck with how perfectly both horses and riders were turned out and how wonderfully they performed. Could she ever ride that well, and possibly, just possibly, have the opportunity to train with them? This became her goal. She got to know the grooms who worked for the USET. She did everything in her power to learn as much as she could, both as a horseman and as a rider, and to ride the best horses she could find. Kathy confided her dream to Theodora Randolph, who had a sharp eye for equestrian talent. Mrs. Randolph purchased High Noon for Kathy to ride. Kathy rode him in the USET trials — and was asked to train with the team! She was only nineteen years old. Then she was invited to ride with them on the fall show circuit. She was flabbergasted.

Kathy Competing On Aberali In Aachen Germany Over A 7'2" Fence

As a result, Kathy was able to train with the team's renowned show-jumping coach, Bert de Nemethy. At Mrs. Dillon's barn, Kathy had learned a pronounced forward seat. De Nemethy wanted her to develop a more neutral seat, so he had her work on the longe line. In longeing, the instructor controls the horse from the middle of a circle, using a long line attached to the horse's cavesson or bridle. This enables the rider to focus on her position. But in her zeal to be the perfect student, Kathy abandoned everything that had gotten her noticed by the USET trainers. Once she started competing, she bombed. She was no longer able to give the horses the sensitive ride she had previously done. After a series of disappointments, which gave Kathy serious doubts about her talent, she decided to return to her roots, to loosen up and ride with the feel she had had before. That did the trick. She went back to riding High Noon, the horse she had ridden in the trials, and finished a close second in two major classes.

She decided to develop her own style, blending the classical training of de Nemethy with the skills she had learned at Mrs. Dillon's barn. This gave her the confidence to continue with the USET and win. She rode with the team for fifteen years and participated in three Olympic Games before she left in 1976.

Being an explorer and a wanderer, Kathy relished the travel opportunities that being on the team afforded. Since she had to maintain amateur status to be eligible to compete in the Olympics, she didn't have the money to travel in style, but this suited her fine. The remuneration she got for her expenses took her to unusual places between competitions. She usually traveled alone and enjoyed learning and experiencing whatever came her way. "I lived inexpensively," she says. "I went to Berlin way before the Wall came down. I didn't fly. I took the train through East Germany. It was great."

Kathy's Renowned Mentors

Although Kathy's own strengths propelled her toward excellence in the equestrian world, she credits several mentors with helping her get there. One of her first as a young equestrienne was Joe Green, a major horse dealer and top rider; he deepened her knowledge of jumpers. The next influential person was Benny O'Meara, a young dealer who was a self-taught genius with horses. Benny had started out in horses without one penny, a condition that Kathy was familiar with herself. Working as a blacksmith, he saved enough money to buy a horse at auction. His business quickly evolved into a big horse-dealing operation and he carried some of the best horses in the country. "He figured it out better than anybody," Kathy said.

Riding with the U.S. Equestrian Team exposed Kathy to some of the best horsemen in the world. The legendary William Steinkraus was a big influence on her. Steinkraus, who captained the team from 1955 until his retirement in 1972, was the first American ever to win an individual medal in Olympic equestrian competition; he was the show-jumping gold medalist in Mexico City in 1968. "Billy was as good as it gets as a rider," Kathy says with frank admiration. "As interesting as it gets as a person. He knew a lot of things and I was very interested in many of them, but I didn't know anything. I'm still interested and still don't know anything ... He always had an audience with me. I was thrilled anytime he wanted to say anything." The two remain close friends to this day.

Kathy Seeks New Challenges

Kathy Kusner thrives on new experiences and the opportunity to develop new skills. At one time, the opportunity to represent the United States in international competitions elated her. As the years went by, though, it became "old news," as she says. Toward the end of her USET career, "on the hunt" for a new challenge, Kathy contacted the Canadian dressage rider Christilot Hanson Boylen, one of the best dressage trainers in North America, whom Kathy knew from their association at the Olympics. Boylen immediately invited her to come to Toronto to train with her for two weeks. "It wasn't dressage *per se*, but training with Christi Boylen that made the difference! A lot of dressage training, as I had experienced it, made you stiff and wooden and the horse too. Obviously this is not what it's meant to do. Boylen brought a wonderful approach and technique to riding, training, and teaching ... The rider's tools made both the rider and horse lighter and more relaxed, but with correct balance, good engagement and energy, happy in their work. Just wished I had learned what she had to offer — earlier the better!"

Even while she was competing at the highest levels of show jumping, Kathy didn't give up her passion for racing. Earlier, after Kathy got out of high school, Theodora Randolph had introduced her to Mikey Smithwick, the expert steeplechase trainer and Racing Hall of Fame rider, who promptly hired her. Smithwick had trained horses for Mrs. Randolph; Kathy's association with Smithwick turned out to be a fruitful one in many ways.

During the USET's off-season, she also got jobs for trainers at Saratoga, the elite New York racetrack. It was there that she got to know the top race rider Angel Cordero. He befriended her and generously shared his wisdom, as Angel always did with new riders. She began to consider whether she could become a race-rider, even though she was a female.

Can a Woman Be a Race-Rider?

In those days young women were much in evidence on the "backside" at the track, exercising and breezing the Thoroughbreds, but there were no women jockeys. The 1964 Civil Rights Act had been passed, however, and gender discrimination in the workplace was now illegal. A woman could not be denied a jockey's license simply because she was female. At least that's what Kathy assumed. She was still busy riding with the USET; surely one of the women who worked full-time at the track would soon step forward and apply for an official jockey's license. But no one did.

Kathy's friend, Dr. Joe Rogers, whose horses she had ridden in local timber races, urged her to go for it. As she was driving back from one of her stints at Saratoga, she decided to accept the challenge, despite her age. "I could get some mounts somewhere, some bad track, here and there, now and then," she mused. "It would be worth it. I'm going to do it."

Kathy's boyfriend in those days was Joe Aitcheson, the leading steeplechase jockey. His first wife had been the attorney, Audrey Melbourne. Kathy asked Joe if she should ask Audrey to represent her. Joe thought that was a great idea. Audrey was such a good lawyer that Joe had hired her to get a divorce from his second wife. Of course Kathy should contact her for this precedent-setting case!

Since Audrey practiced as a Maryland attorney, they had to go to the Maryland Racing Commission, which was notoriously conservative. They didn't like changes. No blacks. No women. Kathy asked Audrey for one favor: Do this quietly. With no press. Audrey responded immediately: no, this is going to be part of our campaign. We're going to get all of the press, including all of the television networks, involved. Kathy gulped. She had never liked speaking to the media. She decided to go ahead anyway.

At the time Kathy could come up with only $1,500. She offered it to Audrey, who refused it, saying, "This will be a landmark decision and I will do it for you for nothing." Every major network featured the plan to bring the case to the commission on the 6 p.m. and the 11 p.m. news. An attorney representing the Marjorie Cook Trust heard the reports and contacted Audrey to offer money to cover Kathy's legal expenses, and then some, for a saddle and other tack that Kathy needed. After generously offering to do the case *pro bono*, Audrey ended up being paid for her efforts.

Audrey Melbourne was an experienced horsewoman and a savvy strategist as well as a seasoned attorney. She also knew the idiosyncracies of the local track people. It took some research to discover what criteria were used to grant jock's licenses. There were no written rules, but the unwritten rules were that one had to go through three hoops: 1) the applicant needed to prove to the starter at the track that she could break a horse from the starting gate, 2) the stewards at the track needed to approve her ability to work a horse in a group of horses on the track, and 3) the easiest part, she had to have a sponsor who was a licensed trainer.

Audrey astutely selected a starter whom she knew loved media exposure. He agreed to evaluate the jock applicant, not realizing that Audrey had appealed to a journalist friend to whom she asked: "Would you like to see history made?" and that this journalist would bring along TV cameramen. He waxed enthusiastic for the cameras, just as Audrey supposed he would. Mission accomplished in test 1! Later, he testified against Kathy in court — but the taped segment that had aired on TV contradicted his testimony.

The next hurdle was to convince the stewards that her riding was up to par; first, however, she had to get them to commit to getting together at one time, a delaying tactic that Audrey and Kathy just waited out. Predictably, given their conservative attitude toward female jockeys, the stewards stated that Kathy was not good enough to ride races. Supposedly she was being turned down for lack of ability, not because of her sex. But both Kathy and Audrey knew that the stewards regularly gave licenses to men with minimal experience, as long as they weighed little enough.

Next, Audrey appealed the steward's decision to the Maryland Racing Commission with all the necessary media exposure that she so carefully choreographed. Here's how Kathy describes the meeting: "The head of the

Racing Commission in Maryland was walking backwards in a circle in his office. I was walking forwards in a circle, holding out my jock's license application. He refused to touch it ... During the next year, I had three hearings in front of the Racing Commission. They had reasons why I couldn't ride races at the track: no changing facilities were available for women; I was an amateur; bettors would not bet on a woman jockey. Of course, the whole reason is that I was a GIRL. They never mentioned that word."

Mikey Smithwick, her guardian angel from her early days as a rider, testified that she was more than adequate to be granted a jock's license, and that the only reason the Commission was denying her was her gender. Even though the major racing journal *The Blood-Horse* railed against the unfairness, the Racing Commission would not change its opinion.

After a year's protracted efforts, since Audrey had exhausted the options with the Commission, she could take the case to court. She demonstrated that Kathy was on a par with others who had been granted a jockey's license, but that she had been arbitrarily barred by the Maryland Racing Commission because she was a woman. Kathy says, "It took thirty seconds for the judge to pronounce, 'You can't deny this person a jock's license.'" As Melbourne said much later, "The Maryland Court determined that the Racing Commission had acted in a capricious, arbitrary, and discriminatory manner based solely on the sex of the applicant."

Just as Audrey Melbourne had predicted, *Kusner v. Maryland Racing Commission* became a landmark case. It opened professional horse racing in the United States to women and was publicized all over the world. As fate would have it, though, Kathy was not the first to take advantage of the newly opened doors. That fall, competing in show jumping for the USET at Madison Square Garden, she broke her leg in a fall and was out of commission for months. Kathy had her jock's license, but she couldn't ride. Diane Crump became the first woman to ride in a race at a major U.S. track, and others soon followed. By the time Kathy was back in the saddle, women jockeys were old news as far as the media were concerned. This was fine with Kathy, a media-shy person. "We were trying to do exactly what the men were trying to do," she says now. "We did not want to be thought of as a female jockey, but as a jockey!"

Kathy admires her younger friend Julie Krone (see Julie's story), who more than any other woman jockey was picked to ride horses in the afternoon races — the ones that count — just like any male jockey. Trainers and owners have chosen Julie to ride their horses in major stakes on a regular basis. This is just what Kathy dreamed would happen as a result of her efforts to legitimize women riding races.

Kathy's Stint as a Professional Race-Rider

Kathy had a hard time getting mounts in the afternoon races because she was by now too old for the all-important apprenticeship weight allowance, called "the bug." Back in 1968, when Kathy was trying to race-ride, the rule was you could get an apprenticeship license from ages 16-26; after that you were no longer eligible for that coveted "bug," or apprentice's allowance.

In a horse race, each horse carries an assigned amount of weight. In some races, all horses carry the same weight; in others, they are "handicapped" according to their previous record. The more weight a horse must carry, the harder it must work to run the course. Thanks to the "bug" the horses that apprentices ride carry less weight; how much less usually depends on how many races the apprentice has won. This gives owners and trainers an incentive to try out an apprentice and it gives newcomers an opportunity to ride some races and try to prove themselves. When an apprentice loses the bug because of age or experience, that incentive disappears. Unless the rider has made a solid impression, mounts will be harder to come by. This was Kathy's dilemma: thanks to the age restriction of twenty-six, she wasn't eligible for the bug, but at the same time she had no winning record to inspire owners and trainers to hire her.

Some trainers came through for her, though, among them her long-time supporter Mikey Smithwick. So did Billy Christmas, a trainer whom she had not known before. Kathy was thrilled, all the more so because Billy quickly put her on all of the horses in his barn, even his best, Terrible Tiger.

While working at the racetrack, she "breezed" a lot of horses (worked them at speed) every morning, hoping that she would catch the attention of trainers who would then name her to ride a horse in an afternoon race. It didn't happen often enough for her to develop the physical fitness required of a day-in, day-out race rider.

"Fitness," she explains, "means that the quadriceps muscles in your legs get so strong that they're not even a thought." But "my legs didn't get strong enough even though I was getting on approximately eighteen horses every morning, which was more than most anybody was getting on. You'd think that would get you fit. Only to a certain level. Not good enough! What gets your legs strong enough is riding four or five races every afternoon." The morning rides helped, but, she says, "With a lot of your morning workers, you're not going as far as you're going in a race. And another thing is, [in a race] you're maneuvering in traffic while you're down low, just living down in that position and then trying to get the most run possible out of the horse through the stretch."

What happened was that people kept bringing "roguey" — tough — horses for Kathy to breeze in the morning. Thanks to her wide experience

Kathy At Julie Krone's House

with difficult horses, she was able to gallop them and work them successfully. But this didn't translate into more competitive mounts in the afternoon races.

Evaluating her own career, Kathy says, "I had an OK racetrack background for a non-jockey, but a very small racetrack life for a jockey." Still, she rode 528 races and won 34: nothing for the record books, perhaps, but she was doing something she loved. "To go to the starting gate 528 times is GREAT!" she says. "It starts with going to the jocks' room well before the races begin, putting on the colors [silks] for what you are riding, and going through the whole process, from the jocks' room through checking your weight on the scales to being thrown up in the paddock, warming up the horse on the track and going to the gate and breaking out of the gate and maneuvering yourself around. It's really, really fun!"

Eventually Kathy got discouraged about the horses she got to ride at the racetrack. "It became the same news, the ratio of how many roguey, rough horses I'd be getting on in the morning as opposed to how many mounts I'd have in the afternoon. Often, none. It's time for another chapter in life. There were more things that were interesting. When you're doing one thing, you're not in a position to do the next new thing, because you're committed to what you are doing. You're nailed to that floor. And you have to get yourself un-nailed."

Kathy Again Challenges Convention – Introduces a Woman to the Maryland Hunt Cup

As if race riding and riding for the USET weren't challenges enough, Kathy decided to enter the Maryland Hunt Cup in 1971. This steeplechase was world-famous for its daunting course and had been considered a "gentleman's" domain since its inception in 1894. No woman had ever dared invade it. The paternalistic officers overseeing the race expressed concerns about women's frailty and the likelihood that the "weaker sex" would get injured on this course, whose solid timber fences are as high as 4' 11". The board of directors balked the night before Kathy was to enter the race. But Turney McKnight, a lawyer on the committee, said they could not legally prevent her from riding. She was a licensed jockey and the 1964 Civil Rights Act would not allow this discrimination. They relented at the last minute.

Mikey Smithwick coached her about the rigors of the course and consulted with the owner-trainer of Whackerjack, the horse she would ride. Of the twelve that started, four horses fell, a common occurrence in this torturous race. Kathy and Whackerjack finished fifth, in a field that included three previous Hunt Cup winners. Not a bad showing for a member of the "weaker sex"!

Kathy Leaves Competitive Riding and Moves to California

In 1979, liberated from her intense equestrian life, owning only what was necessary, Kathy moved to Los Angeles, inspired by a friend, Matt Collins, who was in an acting class there. She was thirty-nine. She found herself enjoying the California lifestyle. She gave clinics, both in the U.S. and in numerous countries around the world; she was showing horses, acting as an expert witness in horse-related cases — and going to an acting class.

She wanted to learn what acting technique was about, not to challenge herself personally, she explains, but to learn a new skill. "It doesn't have to have anything to do with your being good at anything, but if you're interested and curious about it, then the only way to find out about it is to find out about it." She enrolled in a two-year acting class at the Vince Chase Workshop. She took it very seriously. She "prepared like crazy," she says, "because I had no talent at all and I had to work like a fiend on whatever the assignments were. I'd come in very well prepared and do a no-talent job." She wasn't dreaming of becoming a great actress, or even a not-so-great actress. "No," she says, "that wasn't my aspiration. I've never had any problems about not being a legitimate contender in anything. To learn at least something about what you have an interest in is both rewarding and a lot of fun!" It wasn't an acting job, but Kathy had ridden a few years before in the long shots for the Disney movie *The Horse in the Gray Flannel Suit*, so she had had a taste of the atmosphere of the entertainment industry in Hollywood.

Was Kathy so monomaniacal about things equestrian in her twenties and thirties, that she closed out the rest of the world? She was not. In the 1960s she had started taking flying lessons. She couldn't afford to pay cash for the lessons, so she worked out a barter arrangement with some of the horse owners she rode for, first Benny O'Meara and then Mr. and Mrs. Patrick Butler. She became qualified at the highest level as a jet pilot. In the summer of 1973 she became the first woman to fly jets for Executive Jet Aviation, flying the Learjet 23 and 24. She piloted charters and delivered people to places that she would have loved to explore herself, but instead she had to wait to be dispatched to yet another destination. Although she loved flying the jet, the job didn't grab her attention for very long.

Now in her sixties, Kathy is an avid marathoner and ultramarathoner. As of 2008 she had run 108 marathons and 67 ultramarathons. Because she was so intensely involved with horses at the highest levels of competition, leisure riding doesn't appeal to her, but she is still involved in the equestrian world. She earns her keep by giving hunter-jumper and eventing clinics worldwide, teaching privately, and acting as an expert witness on horse-related cases.

Established "Horses in the Hood"

Since 1992 she has been absorbed with Horses in the Hood, a nonprofit organization she started that provides a weeklong riding camp for children from South Central Los Angeles. So far more than five hundred children have learned the basics of riding and horse care and had fun at the same time.

Kathy is enthused about this opportunity to offer inner-city children, some of whom have never seen the Pacific Ocean, a horse experience in a beautiful location, with well-qualified instructors. Housed in Mill Creek Equestrian Center near Malibu, a spotlessly clean eventing barn, Horses in the Hood is funded entirely through donations from old friends in the riding world and from new friends who have heard about the project from newsletters and the website, www.horsesinthehood.org.

The children have instruction in horsemanship for five days. On the fifth day, the program sponsors an event for families and friends, where the camp children demonstrate what they've learned. They are given a disposable camera at the outset and photographs are developed and given to the children at the end of the week. They each get a charming, illustrated book, *Happy Horsemanship* — written from the point of view of the horse — which reinforces the instruction.

Kathy is proud of Horses in the Hood, both for what it has taught hundreds of children and for what it taught her: how to set up a nonprofit organization, get tax-exempt status, develop a board of directors, and raise sufficient funding. She was inducted into the World Sports Humanitarian Hall of Fame in 2005 to commemorate her spirit of giving and the dedication she has had to serve at-risk children and families.

Kathy remains true to her philosophy: Don't nail yourself to the floor, keep options open, and explore new experiences of the mind, body, and heart. Who knows what adventures she'll find for herself as she moves into her seventies?

Carol Kozlowski

Three-Day Event Competitor & Coach

Carol On Good Earth Bit O' Honey At Groton House Farm Horse Trials In Hamilton, MA 2009

If I see a young adult who's passionate, who has the fire in the belly, but not the means, I try to give them a little help. Because I remember what it was like not to have the entitlement, but to have to find a way by means of other people's generosity, to ride.

Carol Kozlowski has made her name — and left her indelible mark — in three-day eventing, a sport in which women weren't even allowed to compete until 1964. In that year Lana du Pont rode on the U.S. three-day event team at the Tokyo Olympics. She fell twice in the cross-country phase but went on to complete the course. The U.S. team won the silver medal. The officials who feared that women were too delicate for this sport must have been shocked. Competing at the Montreal Olympics twelve years later, HRH Princess Anne of Great Britain put three-day eventing on the map.

Intro to Eventing

Today, three-day eventing involves an estimated 14,000 riders in the United States alone, at levels ranging from beginner novice through advanced and on up to the rigors of international competition. Whether a "three-day event" takes place over three days or is compressed into one, it comprises three distinct events: dressage, cross-country, and stadium jumping. Not for nothing is it often called the equine triathlon. The dressage phase — "dressage" in French means "training" — takes place in an arena, or ring. Through a series of precisely executed movements at walk, trot, and canter, it tests the suppleness of the horse, its responsiveness to its rider's aids, and the overall harmony of the horse-rider partnership. In the three-day event, dressage comes first because it helps horse and rider prepare mentally and physically for the next day's rigorous cross-country test (see Jane Savoie's chapter from more information about dressage).

Day two's cross-country phase requires the horse to perform outside on grassy, sometimes wet and muddy fields and demonstrate his speed, his ability to negotiate unfamiliar jumps, and his endurance over difficult terrain. In upper level competitions, the cross-country course generally includes at least thirty daunting obstacles on challenging terrain. Horses must jump over natural fences into water or over piles of logs that require them to land uphill from the obstacle. Horse and rider must be courageous, extremely fit, strong, and in tune with each other to complete the course successfully.

The final test is stadium or show jumping. It demonstrates that even after the demanding cross-country competition, the horse has the stamina to negotiate ten to thirteen colored fences and the tight turns between them.

Recent fatalities and other serious injuries in international competition have focused attention on course design in three-day eventing. Kevin Baumgardner, president of the U.S. Eventing Association [USEA], wrote on their website in the wake of tragedies [March 2008]: "The overall trends [toward more dangerous jumps and terrain] are unmistakable and totally unacceptable." David O'Connor, three-time Olympic eventing medalist and president of the U.S. Equestrian Federation "USEF", puts the dangers in perspective by noting that of 46,099 starters in 2007, only 111, or 0.02 percent, resulted in accidents on the cross-country course, and of these only 10, or 0.002 percent of the total, were serious enough to merit a night's hospital stay.

Carol Tackled the Lead-Weight Problem, a Hazard for Small Horses

As if the sport were not difficult enough, until the very last decade of the twentieth century, smaller riders faced an additional challenge; the FEI "Fédération Equestre Internationale" required horses in international three-day competitions to carry at least 165 pounds. If rider and tack together did not weigh that much, then lead weights would be added to the saddle pad to make up the difference. The rule had been in effect since the early 1900s, when only military men competed in eventing. It had never been challenged.

Carol Kozlowski, standing five-foot-two and weighing 105 pounds, was one who had to add this dead weight to her horse's saddle pad. Concerned about the welfare of her mounts and those of other small riders, Carol set out to get the rule abolished.

At this time Carol was competing the soon-to-be-famous Connemara stallion Hideaway's Erin Go Bragh. At 15.1 hands, Go Bragh is small for an eventing horse, but his suppleness, responsiveness, and courage made up for his size. As he moved up the levels, however, the cross-country courses became ever more demanding. Carol knew that he sometimes faltered under the weight of the extra lead he had to carry. At the 1996 Radnor 3-Day International competition (a challenging course in Pennsylvania), Go Bragh, carrying almost 40 pounds of dead weight, mis-stepped near the end of the cross-country phase and injured his suspensory ligament. Such injuries take a long time to heal and he was out of competition for a year. Go

Bragh's injury solidified Carol's resolve to get this ancient rule changed. In 1991 she had collected the signatures of nine hundred competitors, including such top-level people as the Olympic silver medalist Karen O'Connor, to petition the FEI to change the minimum-weight rule.

But getting the rule changed required much more than circulating a petition. Before the FEI would even consider the request, Carol had to present it to the rules committee of the organization that oversaw equine competition in the United States. This was the American Horse Shows Association, which later became the United States Equestrian Federation, USEF). To Carol's surprise, the rules committee members were unenthusiastic about changing the decades-old regulation, even though the FEI had changed the minimum-weight rule for show jumping back in the 1970s. The committee flatly refused the request, perhaps hoping that Carol would go away. She didn't. Instead, she resolved to procure scientific proof that the added weight was a risk to the horses.

She approached Roger Haller, designer of the 1996 Olympic three-day event course and a member of the AHSA rules committee. Haller was sympathetic to the cause and directed her to Dr. Hilary Clayton, a worldwide authority on equine sports medicine and also a successful eventer. Would Dr. Clayton be willing to conduct a study to determine whether the extra weight had an adverse effect on horses, Carol inquired? Dr. Clayton would, but she estimated that such a study would cost $7,500. Carol set about raising the money. She enlisted the help of her mentor and friend Dr. Joseph O'Dea, former veterinarian for the FEI and the U.S. Equestrian Team (USET). Dr. O'Dea contributed. So did Carol and her husband, Randy, as well as Erin Go Bragh's owners at Hideaway Farm. Others followed. Dr. Clayton agreed to perform the study, even though the amount raised was somewhat short of $7,500.

In May 1995, in Geneseo, New York, home of the Kozlowski's and of Dr. O'Dea, Dr. Clayton simulated the cross-country part of a three-day event. Five horses were tested in ten different trials, some with added weight and some without weight. Dr. Clayton randomly assigned 40 pounds of lead to certain horses and used "retro-reflective markers"—sticky circles placed on key joints that would be bending while jumping. She filmed each trial and reduced the images to computer stick-figures. This enabled her to see which joints were affected and by how much, and to determine the difference between horses that were weighted and horses that weren't. Dr. Clayton spent months analyzing the resulting videos and proved conclusively that horses fared much less well carrying the extra weight and that the risk of injury was serious. "The report was irrefutable," Carol stated. The lead weight made a difference. Now she had scientific evidence to present to the AHSA committee. This time the members paid attention. In 1997 the FEI eliminated the weight requirement.

Carol Was Determined to Get What She Wanted Despite Coming From a Non-Horsey Family

Who is this determined woman and what in her background promoted her perseverance? The second youngest of six children in a musical family in Geneseo, in western New York State, Carol was the only one who was interested in horses. Her parents wanted her to excel in ballet, which she loved. She studied dance from elementary to high school with a small ballet company in nearby Rochester. But she fell *off pointe* and sprained her ankles, a bad omen for a classical dancer.

The experience, however, was not wasted. Says Carol: "That early training in ballet was so useful in the poise, the discipline, the gracefulness, the tenacity, everything you bring to riding. Working through pain. You'd be amazed at how much one discipline is similar to the other. One of my instructors came to watch me ride at a competition in college and she said, 'Oh, now I understand why you're riding, but I see your dancing in your riding.' I thought that was a neat observation."

Her parents and all six children sang and played instruments. All had to learn piano; Carol played flute and piccolo as well. The rest of the family is still active in the church choir, but Carol, because of the intensity of her riding career, is no longer "the church-going girl" she was in her youth. Carol's early immersion in music and dance promoted a sense of rhythm in her riding, especially in jumping and dressage. It is important to know how to hold a beat, she explains. Her experience has given her an edge over other riders by heightening her sense of her own body, where it is, how it feels when she is doing this or that movement on a horse.

Carol's parents supported her in her equestrian activities, but they didn't know anything about the horse world, so they couldn't help her out. As a result, she says, "I had to go the extra mile, frame my own experience. It makes you want it more, a little bit more determined. That's probably why I ended up as passionate in my livelihood involving horses as I did. I had to work my way into it."

Carol was twelve when she started, older than most, but eager to catch up with her cohorts who had started much younger. At fourteen, Carol was working at the local ice cream stand to pay for her lessons. She and her horse-crazy friends jumped, galloped, and fox-hunted—and took more risks than she would consider safe today. With a borrowed horse, she joined the U.S. Pony Club and worked her way up to "A" level. The Pony Club is one of the most respected training organizations worldwide for young horse enthusiasts and one that many high-level equestriennes credit with giving them the basics in English horsemanship. Carol still trains and coaches children in Pony Club.

Pony Club rallies used an eventing format: dressage, cross-country, and show jumping. Early on Carol became adept at all three disciplines and sought out top-level trainers around the country to learn from. Eventing was a young sport in those days, with only about 3,000 people in the U.S. doing it, by official counts. Now the USEA has 14,000 members, and that does not include the eventing enthusiasts who do not participate in USEA-recognized competitions.

Carol found that the more you compete and the more involved you are in the horse world, the more people start to notice you and offer assistance. Dr. O'Dea, a neighbor of her family's in Geneseo, was one of Carol's first mentors. She started working with him before she entered college, continued whenever she had breaks, and even took semesters off to manage his Thoroughbred breeding stable. At the same time she was training with Karen O'Connor (then Karen Lende).

Dr. O'Dea let her ride a three-year-old that he had bred. She trained him, and eight years later he was short-listed for the Olympics. "He became my fairy godfather," she says fondly of O'Dea. Thanks to him, Carol says, "I was exposed to the upper echelons of the sport. After he was the USET vet, he was one of the FEI vets for the World Championships at Lexington [Kentucky] in 1978. I was hired as an assistant to those vets. I traveled to Vancouver, British Columbia, with him for the North American Young Riders Championships and to Baltimore for the World Cup." For a young woman without grand connections, she says, "it was an incredible experience."

Carol's parents were patient with her passion for equestrian activities, but Carol knew that they expected each of their children to earn a college degree. She took a hard look at herself and decided that she really wanted a college degree. She toyed with becoming a vet tech, which would have built on the work she had already done with Dr. O'Dea, but science was not her forte. She did excel in language arts, so she switched her major to sociology. Although the courses weren't hard—she refers to them as "basket weaving"—this was not a major that would lead to a job or a career unless she were to pursue postgraduate study.

At this point, Carol was becoming proficient enough to compete at the upper levels of eventing; this excited her more than her college courses, which partly explains why it took her six years to earn her undergraduate degree—she almost didn't finish her senior year.

With the perspective of more than twenty years now, Carol values her college education and counsels her students to get their degrees. She recognizes the discipline she got as a student, how it broadened and deepened her knowledge about the world, and, especially, how it forced her to develop good work habits. She had to be diligent to "keep all the balls in the air"—being in school, managing O'Dea's barn, and training and competing simultaneously. The skills she developed in college prepared her better for life, she believes, than just working in a barn. "It's a pretty sheltered existence being in the barn all the time," says Carol. Her college education, she believes, has contributed to her success as an equestrian professional. "I'm one of the few who's been talented enough to make a living doing what I do ... you have to be a cut above. It takes a good work ethic."

Carol Was Fortunate to Find Top-Notch Trainers and Horses

While still in college, Carol trained with show-jumping instructor Lynn Klisavage, who was especially impressive with difficult horses. Carol had the passion and the drive, but did she have what it takes to succeed in the professional horse world? Lynn was one of the first pros who told her, "You can do this."

It was through later-to-be Olympic eventer Karen O'Connor that Carol met the Connemara Erin Go Bragh; Karen was riding another

Connemara from Hideaway Farm, right in Carol's hometown. Go Bragh was young and small for an event horse, only 15.1 hands, but Carol quickly recognized his ability and his willingness. Six years after she started riding Go Bragh, the pair was competing at the top levels of eventing.

Erin Go Bragh turned out to be one of the exceptional horses who is talented in all three phases of eventing. The American Connemara Pony Society website describes him in this way: "To watch Go Bragh in the dressage ring is to marvel that this supple, elegant performer is any relation to the shaggy ponies of the west of Ireland ... To see him attack a cross-country course or a stadium round, the catlike grace, the power, the sheer courage of this little stallion are truly evocative of all that is best in his native pony breeding."

Stirlin Harris, a cinematographer and also the son of Jacqueline S. Harris, Go Bragh's owner, approached Carol about making a video of her and her equine partner. The award-winning result, *The Little Horse That Could,* is told from the point of view of the horse and is geared toward young riders who are passionate about competing. Among its accolades are the CINE Golden Eagle, the Parents' Choice Approval, and the Aurora Gold Medal; more than a decade after its release, *The Little Horse That Could* is still selling. "We have a few horses that impact our lives," Carol says now. "He was one of them. He gave me the most notoriety because of the success of this film. If he'd been sixteen hands, it wouldn't have been such a big deal. Everybody loves an underdog."

Go Bragh was retired when he was sixteen. Carol felt that he had given "one hundred-fifty percent"—he was the all-time winningest stallion of any breed in North American eventing competitions—and she wanted to protect him from injury. "I never want to hurt this horse," she told the owners, who were very cooperative about retiring him at the right time. Since then he has proven a successful sire; his more than 200 get already include many proficient eventers. Carol and Hideaway Farms celebrated Go Bragh's twenty-fifth birthday in 2008.

Erin Go Bragh turned out to be the first in a series of wonderful horses that came Carol's way, taking her into more and more challenging competitions. In the early 1980s, when she was in her early twenties, Carol was thrilled to be asked to train with the U.S. Equestrian Team. She rode with the former three-day team coach Jack Le Goff and the eminent dressage coach and judge Jessica Ransehousen. By her own account, she was too starstruck and immature to deal with the pressure of competing with such big-name riders, both her fellow competitors and the trainers. Even though she was long-listed twice, she never made it onto the team. Looking back at the experience, she believes that she was probably too overwhelmed to ride her best. Rather than being devastated about failing to make the team, she told herself that she was young and would have more opportunities in the future.

Carol still saw herself as an unsophisticated country girl from rural New York, but training with the USET was an exceptional opportunity, one she always valued. In the years since, her definition of "success" has expanded. In many people's minds, making the team is the pinnacle of success. For Carol these days, success is more about the quality of teaching she offers her students and the skill with which she trains her horses. "Your parameters change as you get a little wiser," she says.

Carol's Evolution as an Expert Trainer and Upper-Level Competitor

When she rode with the USET, they had just started to videotape training sessions. She remembers being "horrified." She had never seen herself on tape before. She had thought she was doing pretty well, but the tape showed that her body wasn't always doing what she thought it was doing, despite the body awareness she acquired as a classical ballet student. Now there are mirrors around her arena in Geneseo so she and her students can keep an eye on themselves, but she still finds it invaluable to have a person on the ground with a good eye and sound judgment.

She respects and admires Olympic medalist and show jumper Anne Kursinski and numerous other trainers, not only for their coaching and competitive skills, but for their morality and ethical outlook (see Anne's story). Carol believes that to be a good coach one must keep learning and competing oneself. "If you don't stay on top of the learning curve, you're behind," she says. "I don't want my students or riding to be behind because I didn't stay up to speed. I bring what I have discovered or formulated or integrated to these people who haven't had these experiences."

She compares involvement in competition with "being in the trenches." Competition test techniques, training methods, equipment –

everything you go through when competing prepares you to be a better trainer yourself. "You go out and say, 'Well, that didn't work there. Guess I better try this.'" Both she and her students learn from her mistakes and from her successes.

Among Carol's role models as an instructor is Wash Bishop, a respected trainer and former member of the U.S. Olympic eventing team. She had watched him with his students before and admired his quiet, polite demeanor. "He was methodical, level-headed, yet demanding," she says. "He wanted you to try your best and would call you on it." He was confident with students, even the timid ones. "I want some of what you're giving to her (Wash's student)" she told him. "I like to think that he gave me the tools I use now." For several winters, she trained with him at his barns in Middleburg, Virginia, and in Ocala, Florida.

When Bishop stopped training, Carol needed to find another person whom she could respect to keep her learning and progressing in her sport. She found Philip Dutton, an internationally known Australian-born trainer based in Unionville, Pennsylvania. Dutton has become that person on the ground who keeps an eye on her riding, lets her know what she looks like and challenges her to keep learning.

In 2006, Carol had the heartbreaking experience of having a horse she was competing, named Nordic Sparrow Hawk, go lame with navicular syndrome. He had had a successful career at the Intermediate level and she was just about to take him to the Advanced level when she discovered his lameness. She still owns Hawk, who is "very dear to me and will have a home for life."

She knew that Dutton would be able to help her find a new horse, but because he trained so many top-level competitors, she assumed that her needs for a new horse would not be uppermost in his mind. So she got back in touch with Wash Bishop, who had known her for a long time; she knew he had the connections to find horses that could succeed at eventing's upper levels and perhaps they'd be more affordable. Sure enough, Wash was planning a buying trip to Melbourne, Australia within a couple months. Carol went along, and for four intense days, she and Wash checked out horses. He helped her find a "very cool horse," named, comically, "Mr. Snuffleuffagus" better known as "Sniff." Though Philip Dutton is her principal trainer, she enlisted Bishop to help with training Sniff. "We really click as instructor-student," she says. "He's incredibly generous ... just as gifted as he ever was."

Unfortunately, after two years of competing, Sniff went lame by injuring a hind suspensory ligament in the pasture. He had surgery and about a year of lay-up; after nine months of treatment and recovery, he seems to be on his way back to soundness. Carol is bringing him along slowly to build up his stamina. He's back at work now and Carol is hoping that her bad luck with "this cool horse" has run its course and she can compete him again.

Every winter Carol heads south to train with top-level people, taking along three or four horses and a couple of students. For at least six weeks she trains intensively, without the distractions of running a boarding and training stable. She loves "putting my blinkers on," as she puts it, and focusing on her own riding.

Carol has been fortunate in her mentors and trainers. In addition to those mentioned earlier, these include Jane Savoie, who, like Carol, had to make her way to the top of the horse world without money or family backing (see Jane's story).

But Carol also had her share of disappointments, instances where she has trusted someone whose horsemanship impressed her, only to discover that the individual's ethics weren't equal to his or her equestrian skill. "I've had key people in my life treat me unkindly," she says ruefully. "It's always astounding to me when someone you respect or you're loyal to or you hold as a role model will turn around and steal the bread off your plate. It's a competitiveness that is not alien to our business culture. I was a bit naïve in believing you establish these friendships and everyone is going to take good care of everybody else. It's not real. The cutthroat approach to the horse business, when I started running into it, was amazing."

From herself she expects both integrity and generosity. Now she's in a position to do for up-and-coming riders what her mentors did for her. "If I see a young adult who's passionate, who has the fire in the belly, but not the means, I try to give them a little help," she says. "Because I remember what it was like not to have the entitlement, but to have to find a way by means of other people's generosity, to ride ... I didn't have a horse. I took a bank loan out when I was twenty-one years old to buy a racehorse off the track for $600. It was the first horse I ever owned."

Teaching clinics is a particular challenge. In an ongoing relationship, a trainer gets to know her students and their horses very well, their strengths and weaknesses, their personalities, and their learning styles. In a clinic, the trainer is often meeting the horse and rider pair for the first time. She has only a few minutes to assess each one's abilities, diagnose problems, and suggest solutions. "Some people are best when you push on them. Other people just fall apart," she notes. "You have to handle them with kid gloves. You have to be able to integrate all that very quickly and decide what is the most useful way to get them to take a step forward in this experience in a safe, logical, useful manner that everybody benefits from. You've got to be able to generate a little bit of courage by making them believe in what they can do rather than trying to intimidate them into being brave." She's had trainers who believed in the "persecution style" of training: "What are they thinking?" she asks incredulously.

"You have to have a feel for the horse and rider you're dealing with," she emphasizes. "You always want them to come out of the other side of your lesson feeling like they're bigger than they were when they went in. Something magnified in their ability. You don't ever want to

Carol Competing On Take Time, Owned By Lynn Blades At Groton House Farm Horse Trials In Hamilton MA, 2008

diminish people. I've had instructors demean me. I've always said to myself I would never do that. You can be very critical in your instructing and still manage to find a nugget of hope somewhere to leave with that rider."

Carol challenges her students to leave their comfort zone, if only for a moment. She does the same with the horse. If a horse is frightened, she doesn't discipline him. But when he is stubborn, when he signifies he is not going to try a new task, she tells him there is no other option but to do what she asks. For riders to communicate this message to their mounts, they must be confident and mentally prepared.

"You don't approach an exercise with question marks over your heads," says Carol. "You ride with exclamation marks. You say, 'Of course, this is going to happen ... A horse is a herd animal. You have to be the fearless leader. Horses want to know that there is a serious intent. In this sport it's too dangerous for the horse to be throwing in an embellishment of his own. You are running and jumping. You don't want a horse questioning and balking. You can get hurt doing that. Horses can get hurt. You want there to be a full-fledged commitment to the task at hand. 'Throw your heart over the fence, and the horse will follow,' as horsemen say."

No matter what level you ride at, says Carol, choosing the right instructor is crucial. Ask yourself: Do their comments resonate with you? What is their competition history? Whom have they trained with?

Like Jane Savoie, Carol believes that equestrian sports aren't just about winning ribbons in competition; they're about developing a relationship with your horse. Like Savoie, Carol uses imagery to practice riding. She has her students walk a cross-country course first before they compete on it, as she does herself, to feel what they will experience as they are coming around a turn, as they approach a jump, as they leave a jump. They create a virtual ride and rehearse it over and over until it becomes instinctual and they could pick up the ride anywhere on the course.

Also like Savoie, Carol emphasizes the importance of using positive imagery. If you don't, she says, you set yourself up to fail. A mindset riddled with negative images and negative statements can be dangerous to a rider. Instead, you practice saying positive things to yourself and to your horse. And creating images of success.

WHAT'S NEXT? CAROL SAYS SHE HAS A "SENSE OF A WINDOW THAT IS CLOSING" ON HER FUTURE AS A COMPETITOR.

She's not done yet, however; she still has a few challenges she wants to take on. Her current mount—Take Time, called Howie, an Erin Go Bragh son— is talented at all three phases of eventing, so she is not about to retire. Originally, Carol didn't have high hopes for Howie, a fifteen-year-old Connemara-Thoroughbred; as a lower-level competitor, he was difficult and emotional. But when one of her upper-level horses was hurt, she'd load Howie in her trailer and take him to Philip Dutton's for her lessons. He "has so risen to the challenge, it's mindboggling," she says. Howie has become successful at the Intermediate level and she has even competed him at the Advanced level. "He's way beyond my wildest dreams!"

Still, Carol knows she can't do this forever. It's very hard on one's body and she's fifty. When she can no longer compete safely and successfully, she imagines taking on a more administrative role in the equine business. She's already doing some of that. She took over as president of the local Genesee Valley Riding and Driving Club. She "got coerced" into being on the USEA Board of Directors, a serious time commitment that includes several meetings per year plus conference calls. Carol is also a member of a subcommittee of the USEA, called the Professional Horseman's Council. She also intends to keep coaching, training, and judging for as long as she's physically and mentally capable of it.

Carol and her husband Randy — they celebrated their twentieth anniversary in 2008 — have a property with a boarding and training stable. As if the work at home weren't demanding enough, Carol is frequently on the road, training, competing, and giving clinics. Randy, as the East Coast manager for a mortgage management company, also travels frequently for his work, so the two consider themselves lucky when they have more than a couple of days at home with no pressing obligations. Their idea of time off is being together and doing nothing, going to bed early, eating at home and relaxing. Carol loves to read and relishes her solitude.

Randy, whom Carol has known since college, knew what he was getting into when they married; Carol was already traveling extensively to competitions back then. He's a horseman himself; he's particularly passionate about foxhunting and even has his colors with the Genesee Valley Hunt. He also bought a beagle hound pack, called the Roscommon Beagles, from their friend and mentor, Dr. O'Dea; "imagine foxhunting on foot," she explains. The quarry is usually rabbits, but sometimes the young, less experienced hounds will take off on less desirable quarry, much as they do with foxhunting on horseback.

Carol has few regrets about her life thus far. She is thrilled to be doing what she loves best and earning a living doing it. She thinks that she may have limited herself by insisting upon staying in her home base of Geneseo, New York, which isn't exactly the horse capital of the country. But there she's a big fish in a little pond, renowned for her national reputation in the equine world. When her husband was offered a transfer out of the region, she balked. She didn't want to leave her large family, to whom she's always been close, or the community that has been so supportive of her equestrian career. Rather than pull up stakes at this stage in her life, she prefers to make the long treks necessary to train, teach, and compete.

Persistent yet patient with the most junior riders, Carol relishes the role of instructor and coach. Her young riders have earned individual gold and team silver medals in recent years and brought back more medals than in any other area of the country. Equally at home with young riders and green horses as she is with upper-level competitors, she is a versatile equestrienne with an impeccable sense of ethics, a rare combination in a business sometimes driven by individual greed and big egos.

"I try to be honest and straightforward and a little tough in my teaching," Carol says. "I keep expecting and demanding that everybody always give me their best. Always. Every time. Just show me. Just try. Because that's what I'm always doing for everybody else"

Roberta McCarty

Reining Horse Competitor & Trainer

Roberta Competing On Doc N Sasparilla

If you don't have passion, "you're in the wrong business. That's ultimately what draws you to it. You have to have the passion for it, because when it gets hard, there has to be something that keeps you doing it."

Reining star Roberta McCarty pretty much taught herself to ride — and for years she devoted a considerable portion of her time to teaching non-pros how to compete successfully at her favorite sport. Maybe even more inspiring to horse lovers who weren't born into horsey families, she didn't start competing at top levels until she was forty-four in 1994. Since then she moved steadily up the ladder in the competitive arena of the National Reining Horse Association futurities — until she and her husband (who's also her business partner) began to admit to themselves that they were feeling the effects of age and decades of performing in a physically demanding sport. They decided to try out semi-retirement in 2008 at ages almost 58 and 61.

The Sport of Western Reining

What is this sport that has become so popular? Like cutting and other competitive Western horse sports, reining is based on the skills required of the working cow-horse. As a sport it began with informal competitions between cowboys on and off the job. Roberta McCarty and her husband, Jim, didn't start hearing the term "reining horse" until the early 1990s, but they'd long been doing similar maneuvers with their stock horses as amateurs, then as pros. Lead changes, figure eights, rundowns, sliding stops, rollbacks, and spins were commonplace as they earned their way to the top of the Amateur stock division. Roberta explains, "If you want to turn a cow, the horse has to stop the cow, get on its hocks, and roll back to go the other way to get it to where you want it to go. So that would be a 'rollback.' The rollback evolved into a sliding stop and then rolling back. The rollback is a 180-degree change of direction by the horse at the end of a sliding stop. It's well done when the horse uses its hocks low to the ground with quickness and ease."

In the United States, reining competition is overseen by the National Reining Horse Association (NRHA). The pinnacle of the NRHA's season is the futurity, a two-week-long event held from Thanksgiving through early December in which more than four hundred horse-and-rider pairs compete for a million dollars-plus in prize money — the winner goes home with $125,000. The total purse for all winners for that show is over $1.5 million. Currently, most of the NRHA's members are in Texas and California, but reining is gaining popularity in the eastern part of the United States and Canada — and overseas as well. It is the first Western discipline to be sponsored by the United States Equestrian Federation, the national governing body for U.S. equestrian sports. In Europe these days huge crowds turn out for international reining competitions.

Roberta Learned Horses on Her Own

No one in Roberta McCarty's family knew much about horses, but from a young age she immersed herself in TV Westerns and preferred toy horses to baby dolls. Outside, like many other horse-crazy young girls, she'd play at being a horse. She grew up in suburban Orange County, California, having moved there from Ohio as a youngster. On one memorable visit back to Ohio with her parents, she rode horseback for the first time. "I must have been nine or ten," she recalls, "and I took off on a horse. I didn't know how to, and it was this feeling that you're in control and you're free. I don't know how I knew how to ride a horse."

Roberta begged her parents, the late Anne and Robert Zehner, to get a horse, to no avail. She hung around local boarding stables, looking for opportunities to ride. Finally, someone pointed to a horse and said, "If you can catch that horse, you can ride him." She managed to do it. At last her parents succumbed to her pleas; they bought that horse for her, named Pancho, sometimes called Pancho Lopez, for $500. They paid for board, but there was no money left over for a saddle, so she rode bareback, developing balance and a good seat in the process.

Her parents enrolled her in 4-H, where she learned both horse care and basic horsemanship. With the other horse-crazy kids, she would race up and down the levees and jump. It turned out she had a competitive streak. When she heard someone else had jumped her horse three feet, Roberta had to do better — all without a saddle. "I was stupid fearless," she says, looking back. She competed at informal shows and won her share of ribbons, which the children made themselves. Those homemade ribbons still hang alongside the fancy ones she's won at top NRHA events. "They remind me where I started," she says.

Roberta's parents decided it would be cheaper to buy a horse property than to keep paying board, so they moved to Riverside, California, a rural area not far from where the McCartys ranch is now. By then her dad was hooked on horses, too; he had begun to buy inexpensive Thoroughbreds and race them at tracks like Caliente in Tijuana, Mexico. Her mother, however, was always terrified of horses and avoided even walking them on a lead line.

Roberta's Family – "Good Honest Working People"

Roberta's parents, Anne and Bob, were high school sweethearts, but since her dad wasn't ready to settle down, her mother married someone else. When he came back from World War II, the spark was still there. She got divorced and the two finally married. Both of the Zehners worked hard all their lives, he as a machinist and she making computer circuit boards. They never had any extra money. "They were just good honest working people," says their daughter. She remembers her father as a perfectionist, much like herself, and handy, like her husband, Jim. She and her mother often clashed. At the time Roberta believed her mom favored her half-sister, Linda, who was eight years older and "more of a girly-girl." In retrospect, she believes she and her mother butted heads because they were too much alike. Both were assertive and opinionated, in contrast to her dad, who was "like milque-toast." Her dad lived into his mid-eighties, outliving all his siblings. Her mother succumbed in her mid-seventies to a smoking-related illness.

Roberta's parents didn't always see eye-to-eye, but they were committed to each other and their commitment influenced their younger daughter. "When I commit to something, I commit to it," she says, "and it's real hard for me to quit." Today, as a ranch owner, she appreciates loyalty in her employees and finds it hard to fire someone even if they are not doing a good job.

"Horses are Good Life Lessons"

Roberta brought to her horse life a dedication that she never felt for academics. Every day after school she was at the stable, taking care of her horse. The lessons she learned there have stayed with her all her life. "I always tell people that horses are just like life," she says. "One minute you could be enjoying everything and the next minute the horse goes lame. Horses are good life lessons for children. They teach you responsibility. They can teach you to be competitive. They can teach you how to win and how to lose."

They also taught her how to teach herself. She didn't have a trainer or regular instructor, so she learned by trial and error and by seeking out books about horses and horsemanship. Reading about the Lippizaners of the Spanish Riding School made her wonder how to teach a horse to do a capriole, an advanced "above the ground" movement in which the horse leaps into the air and kicks out with his hind legs. "One day," she recalls, "I was doing something stupid with my horse and he leaped in the air and I'm thinking, 'Aha, this is cool.' So I'd take him down to the arena and I would run him back to the end of the gate. I would do that five times in a row to where he'd get excited to go back in the gate. Then I'd take him to the end of the arena and I wouldn't let him run. I'd hold him and he would leap through the air. That was a capriole."

Once a woman who recognized her talent offered to introduce her to a good trainer. "I was so looking forward to it," Roberta says, but "the woman was involved with this guy, and she ended up killing his wife, literally shooting her in a bar. And went to jail for it. So that didn't work. The reason that sticks in my mind is because it was going to be my first foray into actual structured teaching."

If she had had mentors and coaches, Roberta thinks she would have been more successful earlier in life. "I had to figure it all out by myself," she says now. "I tell people it's like this maze to go through. When you're on your own, you're going to hit a lot of walls. But when you have someone who's guiding you, you're going to be able to maneuver through this maze, and it's going to be a lot clearer in your mind. So I would advise people to get someone to help them."

Post-High School – Roberta Starts to Blossom

After graduating from high school, Roberta took the Civil Service exam and got her first job in a naval weapons department, first as a secretary and later in the travel office. Roberta hated being cooped up inside all day. She didn't last long at that administrative job. As soon as she could, she quit to try to support herself in something she'd like better.

Aside from horsemanship, Roberta was known by people in her community for her singing. Early on her mother saw that she was interested in singing and could carry a tune, so decided she must have singing lessons. She remembers being taught light opera, which wasn't very appealing to a pre-teen. She entered a local contest and got a raging cold just in time for the competition. But her singing talent led to choral groups as she got older, including the high school Madrigal Group which she had to audition for. It was an honor to be chosen. She remembers her high school mentor, the choral director, Mr. Halperin. "He didn't put up with crap, but if you worked your ass off and were passionate about the music, you and he would get along just fine." She thinks she learned something about teaching and coaching from Mr. Halperin, who concentrated on fairness, respect, and discipline, which she applied later to her teaching methods.

Towards the end of high school, Roberta sang lead with a trio of girls. They'd go to senior residences, called "old age homes" in those days and to small business groups, and through this experience, she developed a "personality," rather than being the shy and retiring girl she was at a younger age. She had to stand up in front of strangers and come up with amusing anecdotes. The group even recorded a demo tape in Hollywood for someone who was looking for the next Mamas and Papas. No, it was not them.

Roberta was also beginning to be known for her horsemanship. She started giving lessons one night a week by her late teens or early twenties. Ten or twelve people would come, so she must have already made a name for herself. Now she can't imagine what she taught or how she had learned it. She thinks it was mostly from books by people like William Steinkraus, the Olympic show jumper.

She started training Appaloosas at the barn of a friend of the family named Liz Phelps. She developed her own skills in a variety of equestrian disciplines, including Western pleasure, trail riding, jumping, hunter hack, and showmanship, and taught them to children and adolescents. What she lacked in formal training, she made up for in talent and passion. If it hadn't been for a certain innate aptitude, she probably wouldn't have been able to learn so much with so little assistance. And if you don't have passion, "you're in the wrong business. That's ultimately what draws you to it. You have to have the passion for it, because when it gets hard, there has to be something that keeps you doing it."

Marriage to Jim – Partners in Life and Work

In her early twenties, Roberta met Jim McCarty, an expert farrier who shod most of the good stock horses in southern California. It wasn't love at first sight. He was so shy and quiet, she thought he was boring. She began to see a different side of Jim and they married when she was twenty-four.

"You would never have heard my name if I hadn't married that man," she says. Throughout their long marriage and business partnership, he has encouraged her to promote herself in professional circles. His steady income as a farrier helped compensate for the financial ups and downs as Roberta established herself as a trainer and competitor.

Not only is Jim an excellent horseman, he's adept at the myriad tasks required on a working ranch, where something's always needing to be built or bought or repaired. Jim "can read anything and comprehend more than I can," Roberta admits. For example, "Neither one of us ever used computers, so one day, about fifteen years ago, he bought a computer. He'd never touched a computer. He brought it home in a box, set it up, and was working the computer that night, and I didn't even know what a mouse was."

I asked Roberta if they had ever considered having children. She responded that they had thought about it years ago, even read all the books. "Being such a perfectionist and a committer ... One of my pet peeves is people who have children and then ignore them. I could never have done that. With me, if you have a kid, that's what you do, you spend your life turning out a productive, compassionate member of society to the best of your ability. We got to a point in our lives where we were really busy, we had the horses, we had the ranch, and we were content. It's like, "okay, time for kids!"

They asked each other, "Do you really want kids?" and both answered, "No." She regrets, however, that she didn't have the opportunity to be a parent, because she sees that having children develops tolerance and patience. Both she and Jim could use more of that. She also worries about what they will do with "all the crap" that they have accumulated. Material objects became less important to them, she thinks, because they'll have no children to be sentimental about the things they have treasured. She showed me an old cowboy reata, the rope cowboys used to catch cows, but is sad that they won't have offspring who will value these pieces.

The two complement each other. Roberta is more single-minded and competitive; Jim, who once seemed so shy, is more well-rounded and outgoing. Being partners in business as well as in life is rarely easy, but both have risen to the challenge of making it work. Over the years each has learned when to push and when to step back. Jim "recognizes my talent and tries to guide me," says Roberta, "but there is a point where you're unguidable. We both get to that point and instead of keep hashing at it, we just let it go. I think that's part of commitment. If you're just going to butt heads, and each person has to be right 100 percent of the time, it's not going to work."

Both Roberta's determination and Jim's knowledgeable support were crucial as they made the transition from training and showing stock horses to the more exacting sport of reining. Roberta's first forays into reining competitions were less than impressive, and no wonder. There was a lot to learn.

The Sport of Western Reining

Like their dressage counterparts, reining competitors are expected to be in near-perfect control of their mounts as they execute one of ten patterns, each of which comprises a number of precise maneuvers, including small slow circles, large fast circles, flying lead changes, rollbacks over the hocks, 360-degree spins in place, and sliding stops. Each contestant performs the same pattern.

Here is a description of Pattern 1 (of ten distinct patterns)
as found in the NRHA Guidebook:

- Run at speed to far end of arena and do a left rollback.
- Run to opposite end and do a right rollback.
- Run past center and do a sliding stop. Back up to center and hesitate.
- Complete 4 spins to the right and hesitate.
- Complete 4 ¼ spins to the left and hesitate.
- On left lead, do 3 circles to the left; 1st is large and fast;
  2nd is small and slow;
  3rd is large and fast. Change leads at center of arena.
- Complete 3 circles to the right: 1st is large and fast;
  2nd is small and slow; 3rd is large and fast. Change leads at center.
- Begin large fast circle to the left but do not close this circle.
- Run up right side of arena and do a sliding stop.
  Hesitate to demonstrate completion of the pattern.

Each rider starts with 70 points. For each maneuver within a pattern, the judges add or subtract points in half-point increments. A flawless performance might earn 1.5 points; a disastrous one might lose the same amount. Roberta explains: "If you do a spin and you do it correct and fast and your horse is quick and willing and it's right in the spot it needs to be in, they're going to give you a plus, maybe a plus one (upping your score to 70.5 or 71). If you do that spin and it's hoppy and ugly and the horse is flipping its head and looking out of control, then you lose one to one and a half points (decreasing your score to 69 or 68.5)." If your performance merely meets criteria, then your score remains a 70. Certain infractions — such as spurring in front of the cinch or using the hand to punish or praise the horse — incur a five-point penalty. Perfect scores are theoretically possible but unheard of in practice. It is difficult for horse and rider to flawlessly execute all of the seven or eight maneuvers in a pattern. Adding speed to the patterns, yet doing them with style and precision, will enhance the score.

It takes a trained eye to perceive and appreciate the subtleties of reining, which is why Roberta does not expect it to become a great spectator sport in the United States. Jumping, for instance, is both exciting and easy to understand. It offers the "crash and burn" sensation that audiences love. "You get over a jump, and you win. Knock one down, you lose." Nevertheless, the sport of reining is growing in popularity and not just among Western riders.

Judging is inevitably somewhat subjective, so at large events there are three judges. At the NRHA Futurity, there are five, and the high and low scores for each ride are thrown out. Roberta's personal best from three judges is 226.5.

Here Roberta's perfectionism — which she considers a mixed blessing — made a big difference. Perfectionism, she says, "definitely helps you in the reining, but it will drive you nuts. You don't have to be loony tunes about it, but if you're not somewhat of a perfectionist, you probably won't be any good at it, because it does require a lot of drilling and a lot of repetition. It can be a little mundane at times. Sometimes I get tired of looking at the ground, making a circle. If you want things to change every day, it is not going to happen."

In little more than a decade Roberta McCarty went from "rookie trainer" status — meaning she hadn't won any money in competition — to a place on the 2006 Top 20 Professionals List; that year she won a total of $56,000. As of January 2007, she was reining's top pro female moneymaker with a career total of $278,000. Horses that can compete at the Open level

— the summit of pro competition — are rare. "I'm looking for a Secretariat every year," Roberta said. They don't come cheap either. A two-year-old with the potential to go to the top might sell for between $165,000 and $200,000, but since such horses haven't been trained or tested, it's a gamble as to whether they'll actually make money.

In this sport, even non-pros earn money, but not nearly as much prize money is available in their divisions. Few non-pros are able to compete against professionals, in large part because of their attitude, rather than their talent. Pros, Roberta explains, take winning very seriously; they want to achieve a goal, whereas non-pros do it more for recreation. Pros have to be completely consistent in their training and riding. "Pros love the horses, but don't fall in love with them to a point where they can't make business decisions that will take them to their goal." Non-pros, she notices, will stick with a horse even though that horse isn't particularly suitable for their riding level or for reining competitions. "Eighty percent of the time non-pros will continue with the horse they have and complain about not being competitive."

Roberta used to dream of becoming the first woman to win the NRHA Futurity. She made her first big futurity final in the Limited Open in 1994, when she was forty-four. "I just grinned as I walked into the ring. Imagine my thrill to find myself in a position to be a woman at that age competing in my first big NRHA Final."

She got the futurity bug after that and bought a 2-year old prospect for a client, the hunter trainer legend, Hap Hansen. They proved a lucky team and she made the Limited and Open Finals on his 3-year old, Freckles Bar Mister, in 1997. She admits, "I would proudly put my earnings record next to many of the original reiners since I got such a late start." Since then she has been in the NRHA Open Finals four times, more than any other woman; twice she was the only woman in the Open Finals. As of 2008, Roberta was still the #1 Professional NRHA female lifetime money earner, although she expects her record to be surpassed soon, as she's not showing in 2008.

"So be it", she says, "I have no regrets. I am surprised every time I see my name on the leading money earner lists, and it makes me smile." Even though she believes that a woman can make top scores in a futurity, she believes it's a young man's sport, because it's so physical. To date, no woman has had more NRHA Open Finalists than she has. "I thank God every day that I was able to find a talent and get the most out of it. I have had a lot of people and horses that have contributed to my career and I appreciate every one of them."

"The only thing holding a woman back is a great horse," she believes. "The time is right for a woman to jump up and get the top spot at the futurity. No woman has ever won it." That was a goal she had had for herself. She was confident that she could have accomplished that, if she could have found the winning horse. But, that was the hard part. "When you get to my level, you need those kinds of horses, and they don't come along very often."

Unless you're already at the top, wealthy horse owners don't show up in your barnyard begging you to train their expensive two-year-olds. So Roberta was always searching for a horse with a champion's attributes: quick and athletic, good-looking, with the right conformation and attitude. "There are women in this country capable of winning the NRHA futurity," she told an interviewer in 2003, "but are they getting that kind of stock?" She also mused about whether women competitors, including herself, might be hampered by their own attitudes. Top male reiners exude confidence, but, Roberta admits, "I don't go to a horse show thinking, 'I'm the greatest thing since sliced bread, and I'm going to kick every body's butt.' I never think that. If I don't kick somebody's butt, then I'm pissed at myself. I take defeat hard. I'm hard on myself."

And even if you do get that rare horse who can go all the way, there are no guarantees. "It's the horse," Roberta says. "It's the judges. It's the crowd. It's the luck. And it all has to come together in one four-minute deal. That's the part you have no control over. The only part you have control over is the homework you've done and the product that you put out there."

Musing About their Reining Business and Moving On

The McCartys had built a thriving business, buying, breeding, and training reining horses, coaching youth and non-pro students, and competing their own and others' top-level reining horses. The McCarty Ranch is located in wine country near Temecula, north of San Diego, where the terrain is hilly with mountains in the distance. Here on these five acres Roberta and Jim McCarty devoted themselves to the business of training and competing high-level reining horses.

Now that they are experimenting with more leisure, spending six months of the year at their condo in Maui, Hawaii, Roberta has time to look back and review their years running the ranch, competing, training others' horses and her own. Now she is taking pleasure in not having a rigid schedule, in traveling to re-connect with old friends. She described what her days were like just a year ago.

Roberta On Chexy Dun It, 2004

Preparing for major competitions used to involve two or more weeks of sixteen- to eighteen-hour days. Not so long ago, Roberta might have hauled at least twenty, and maybe as many as thirty-two, horses to a show. Then she realized that if she took fewer horses, she'd be more relaxed and have time to socialize with old friends. Like many competitors, both she and her husband enjoyed the camaraderie of seeing the same people, year after year, at shows across the country.

But setting limits can be a challenge, as Roberta explains: "The trouble with the horse training business is, you want to keep it at a manageable level. What happens when you say you're full and this guy calls you and he has the best horse on the planet? Well, you're going to take it. You're not going to say 'I'm full,' because you don't know if one of these other guys is going to leave. Maybe they're going to go into boat racing, you don't know. So, you take all that you can handle" because you never know when someone is going to leave.

After successfully showing in non-pro classes in California until 1980, Roberta and Jim began their training business in 1981. They coached non-pros and competed in Western pleasure, trail, and stock horse classes. Eventually they decided to relinquish all their other interests and concentrate on reining. Roberta started buying or boarding others' two-year-old horses, training them for a year, and then competing them at the futurity if they showed promise.

Mentors and Role Models

Even though Roberta is largely self-taught, she acknowledges the importance of mentors and role models in her own life. Liz Phelps, an old family friend, who may have passed on now, was such a mentor. Liz came into her life when she was sixteen; Roberta rode Liz's Appaloosas for several years, until her early twenties. Liz gave Roberta her first horse job that actually paid well. But, life didn't proceed so well for this friend and mentor. "Liz gave up every creature comfort to be with the horses and ended up penniless." Roberta realized that was not a goal for her. She wanted to make a business out of her love of and talent for horsemanship. "Luckily," Roberta says, "I married a smart man so together he and I could build a financial future outside of the horses... We stayed out of debt and invested in real estate so now we are able to take the time to enjoy ourselves ...

Sometimes you learn valuable lessons from people that they don't even realize they are teaching you!"

But Roberta valued her association with Liz Phelps, who was instrumental in urging Roberta to show horses. "She really got me pointed in the direction of competitive showing and gave me some horses to ride. I had talent. I didn't know what to do with it. She recognized that and tried to channel it."

Penni Gerardi, a horse trainer and good friend now, was another major influence on Roberta's horsemanship. Penni was at the top of her sport when clients got her into reining. She brought reining to Roberta's attention. "[She was] somebody who accelerated my career."

Dick Pieper was a reining legend in Oklahoma. She met him briefly when he exhibited top reining horses in California, early on in her career. She thought he was wonderful, a great ambassador for the sport. He was the type of guy whom you wouldn't see for a few years and then you'd run into him and he'd remember your name. She went to Oklahoma and rode with him in 1994 for a week and she still contacts him when she has questions. "He opened my eyes to reining. He gave me light-years of experience, and I don't think he even knows ... Just being around him, his mental attitude. He's a very upbeat person. Everything he did was so different from the way we did it here. He was less precise than I thought one had to be to get the desired look on a reining horse. He taught me to think out of my box, not to be afraid to make a mistake, to let the horse make a mistake at home so you could teach it the right way. His riding demonstrated how to get the horse "between the reins,' a necessary thing when you are running fast and directing the horse where to go next."

Ronnie Richards was another role model for Roberta. He was a great stock horse trainer whom Jim had worked for as a farrier. He and his wife Karin have become good friends. "The man was incredible. He's a true gentleman and horseman. He's retired now, but he was the greatest stock horse trainer that ever walked out here. Anytime I want I can call him up and say, 'I'm having a problem with this,' and we talk.

Roberta as Trainer-Coach for Non-Pros and Pros

Adult and youth non-professionals made up about 90 percent of Roberta's business. With her clients, she was not judgmental as she has been about her own performance. When they felt they were letting her down, it broke her heart. "What are you talking about?" she told them. "You went in there and did the best you could do. If you didn't win, that doesn't matter."

She took her teaching seriously; she carefully observed the cognitive and emotional needs of her students. She thrived on the inspiration she got from students who are excited to learn about reining. When she worked with young people, she made conscious use of her skills as a "communicator, mentor, and authority figure," knowing that these would have an impact on her students — much as they do on young horses. The youth reiners are more accustomed to taking direction from a teacher or parent and less likely to question an authority figure. Roberta wanted to be a role model not only as a successful rider and instructor, but also as an ethical business-person and someone who shows compassion for the horses. She hoped that these young people would be able to draw on these lessons for the rest of their lives. So she always treated her youth clients with respect and never belittled or degraded them.

Coaching the adult non-pro is a different matter. Her adult clients often were high-functioning professionals or entrepreneurs. They had another life in which they excelled. They made time for reining because it's fun and challenging. Roberta had to respect their needs and their time constraints. Unlike the youth, they did question her. They expected to be given answers. They were more accustomed to giving orders than to taking them. Often they've forgotten what it's like to be naïve and awkward, when the mind understands what to do, but the body takes a while to catch up.

When I first met Roberta, she told me that she expects that she'll keep training riders long after she's stopped competing herself. She has the excellent eye and long experience that make a good teacher. She coached her younger assistants, Amy Walden, the woman who is now running the show when her boss is in Maui, and Robin Killiany, as they rode ten or twelve horses every day. Until she and Jim decided to try out semi-retirement, she still rode four to eight horses a day, physically demanding work, especially with young horses. As they made the decision, "a sea change" for them, they wondered, how much longer can we put in the physical and mental labor of running the business and competing?

"I'm really enjoying not having the pressure of clients and competition for the first time in nearly thirty years." But it's strange for them to make travel plans without consideration of the horses. Fortunately, Roberta's diligence in training her young staff is paying off. She has full confidence in leaving them to run the business.

It's especially gratifying for Roberta, who is largely self-taught, to have mentored her staff and to see how professional, ethical, and skilled they are. These are the attributes she valued most highly in the people she looked up to as a young competitor on stock horses. Now she gets compliments from professionals she respects about Amy and Robin. "They are courteous, patient teachers, good to the animals, and very competitive, at the top of the limited Open division, by a landslide." So, perhaps Roberta's goal of becoming the first woman to win the Futurity is being transferred to one of the young women whom she so lovingly has coached for the past few years.

What's next? This dedicated and talented horsewoman has steadily climbed the ranks of winning competitions, even though she didn't start competing in reining until her mid-forties. Now she is enjoying the fruit of her labors, slowing down, and relishing the thought that the young women she has trained may someday achieve the top level in the Futurity that she coveted just a few short years ago.

Karen Womack Vold

Trick Rider & Trainer

Karen Performing Side Somersault Drag With the Fireballs, At Sidney, Iowa Rodeo 1961

"I have great perseverance, a no-quit philosophy. But it can verge into stubbornness. I'm more willing to stick my neck out when it comes to defending my brood, whether it's children or horses. Then I take action and can fight like a banty rooster."

From the Vold ranch in rural southern Colorado, Pikes Peak is visible far off in the distance; even in June it's covered with snow. The house was built after the Civil War, before Colorado attained statehood. Its original owner brought all the necessary lumber with her from St. Louis on a horse-drawn wagon, along with her fancy china and linens. The well-appointed homestead in the middle of a largely uninhabited prairie became an elegant meeting place for nineteenth-century Western notables. When Karen and Harry Vold bought the house, its former splendor was largely forgotten. "Nobody had lived here for seven months and so the pipes all froze up and broke," Karen recalls. "There was no refrigerator. There was no toilet that worked. And so we started getting little things fixed. It's well worth the fixing up, but if I had had enough foresight, I would have taken those pictures of the before and after."

The Vold's transformed the property into a comfortable ranch including house, barn, riding arena, and pastureland for seven hundred top-quality stock horses who graze on twenty-thousand acres. The 130-year-old house now includes a fully equipped gourmet kitchen. Karen loves to cook so much that she's self-published *Spurs & Spoons Cookbook: A Buffet of Memories from Karen's Collection*, based on recipes she's collected for years from rodeo friends. Favorite recipes, such as Baked Apple Pie Dumplings, Tami's Soft Taco Casserole, or Crock Pot Cheesy Creamed Corn were designed to feed the crowds that they sometimes have at the ranch when they host clinics.

It's clear from almost every room that the Volds are a horsey family. The house is handsomely decorated with saddles, belt buckles, lassos, framed awards, and photographs of family members performing on horseback.

Harry Vold is a successful stock contractor for rodeos in the United States and Canada. The couple breed and raise pure black horses with a white blaze, their signature breed; they train them to be bucking horses for rodeo. For decades their lives have revolved around the business of supplying stock to rodeos as much as five hundred miles from home. They're on the road most of the year, it's a grueling life, but one they both love. Harry Vold started supplying stock to rodeos when he was a teenager and he's still going strong at eighty-one. Even though the Volds' youngest daughter, Kirsten, has taken the lead in running the business now, one of the only women who plays this role in rodeo, Karen and her husband still trailer the horses to every rodeo and are an integral part of the scene.

Karen's Growing Up Years Weren't Easy

Karen was born in 1939 in Phoenix, Arizona, the first of three children. Her parents, Andy and Ruby Elizabeth McCauley Womack, were involved with rodeo from the time she was a baby. Both were active in the JayCees, the organization that put on the Phoenix rodeo every year. Karen was the mascot for the wives' branch, called the Dudettes, when she was two years old. In spare time when not too busy with his construction business, her father chaired the rodeo to keep it going during three of the years of WWII; he was the only person ever to chair for more than a year. Rodeo clown celebrities, George Mills and Jasbo Fulkerson, were regular house guests from the time Karen was a youngster. Jasbo died when she was eight in a tragic truck accident, while driving home from a rodeo; having learned to be a barrel clown from his friend, her father took over Jasbo's rodeo acts. The rodeo environment enthralled Karen, but being an agile, athletic girl, it was the trick riding that grabbed her attention, not the clowning that her dad's friends did.

At her mother's insistence, she started dancing lessons at the age of three. She loved to perform, to hear the applause, to know she did a good job. Her earliest ambition was to become a professional ice skater, a trapeze artist, or a trick rider; in her world, skating rinks and circuses were harder to come by than rodeos, so trick riding won out.

In school she played basketball, softball, and track. She had to build up her forearms for trick riding, so would do chin-ups and push-ups on the advice of her riding trainer. She was also an avid swimmer. The cement irrigation channel that watered the family's citrus groves was the swimming hole where local kids congregated during the hot Arizona summers; Karen's father furnished it with a diving board and a swing. The children never changed out of their swimsuits, even to sleep. They'd sleep on the roof, where it was cooler, then every morning before breakfast, they'd crawl through the oleander bushes and dive into the swimming hole.

Even as a young girl Karen would confidently guide trail rides out into the desert at her parents' riding stable. For several years Karen's twin cousins, who were almost exactly her age, lived with the family. They dressed alike and fooled people into thinking they were triplets, but she was the only one of the trio interested in riding.

When Karen was eight, her parents divorced. She was devastated.

She blamed alcohol for the demise of her parents' marriage, so has never touched it herself. After the divorce, her father gave up his construction business and took off on the rodeo circuit. Karen, who was never close to her mother, wanted more than anything to join her dad, but both parents agreed that the rodeo was no place for a young girl. So for six years Karen didn't see much of her father. Both of her parents remarried several times, so she accumulated a number of stepsiblings, but she never took a liking to any of her stepparents. "When you're a kid growing up and you have lots of problems and stepparents that you don't like, you got to have a friend, so my friend was my horse," Karen says now. "I would tell him all my problems and I would go off and ride and get away."

Despite her horse friend and a strong private relationship with God, she grew angry and morose. Worried, hoping to distract her from her depression, her parents decided to pool resources and buy her a horse who'd been trained for trick riding, as well as a trick-riding saddle. Karen was already trying to copy the trick riding she had seen at rodeos, standing in the saddle with one foot or standing in the stirrup, but using a regular Western stock saddle. That made the tricks much more challenging. On a specialized trick-riding saddle, the horn is about seven inches tall, so the

Trick Riding Saddle From Karen's Collection

rider can grip it with both hands. The seat and cantle are flat with handholds on the back. The more straps a trick rider has to use, the less experienced is the rider; Karen soon learned to do tricks with few straps.

There are three categories of tricks on a horse: topwork, including standing on top of the saddle, vaults, where you hit the ground with your feet and vault back onto the saddle, and strapwork or drags, where you grasp holds on the saddle and hang near the ground on the side or back of the horse. The back drag, one that the famous Tad Lucas did, is the most difficult. You hook your feet into straps on the rump of the horse and hang your head over the flying feet of the horse.

Says Karen about Gold Dust, the first trick riding horse she owned: "[The horse] was a stallion at the time and the woman used to jump a car as well as trick ride on him. But some of the time [when riding a pair of horses, one foot on each, as in the 'Roman stand'] he would refuse to jump and the other horse would jump and she would fall, so they agreed to sell the horse to my dad. He was already broke for trick riding. Because I was a little girl, my dad was afraid of the horse's being a stud, so he had him gelded." Presumably, he was more compliant once he was gelded, as Karen had no horror stories of her own childhood accidents on this horse.

When Karen was ten, Louise "Tex" Lee, who trick-rode a beautiful palomino named Golden Eagle, came to work at the family stable. Tex taught her the three tricks she knew: the Cossack drag, the Hippodrome stand and the One-foot stand. In the Cossack drag, you hang upside down with one foot across the horse and the other up in the air; "it's easy to learn," Karen says. In the Hippodrome stand, you have your feet in straps on the saddle and stand up on a fast cantering horse. In the 1-foot stand, you stand on one leg, "ice-skater stance" with the other one raised in back of you. "I used to do them up and down the canal bank that bordered our riding stable," Karen says,. "And that's where I began my trick riding."

Meanwhile, Karen's father, Andy Womack, had teamed up with the bullfighter George Mills, replacing their deceased friend Jasbo; the "bullfighter" is the one whose job it is to distract the bull to keep the cowboy safe. Andy took on the role of the barrel clown on the rodeo circuit. The barrel clown's job is to protect the cowboys after they are thrown off a bull or when they dismount after the requisite eight minutes. They distract the bull with their antics and bright colors, thus entertaining the audience while protecting the cowboy riders.

Womack had learned rodeo clowning from his old friend Jasbo, who had also invented a barrel made of heavy-gauge steel and lined with foam rubber. Part of the clown's act might involve jumping in and out of the barrel — while dodging the horns of an angry 3,000- or 4,000-pound bull. "The stock contractor tries to pick a bull that likes to hit the barrel," Karen explains. "And there's some bulls that will and some that won't. My dad's in the barrel and the barrel goes end over end, and that's what the people like. Nowadays the clown just puts a stick or a broom behind him. It's just a dummy, like a scarecrow, but when my dad was clowning, he used to run a wire across the arena and had a dummy hanging off. This chimp he trained was fastened on the dummy and he would shake the dummy to get the bull's attention. The bull would hit the dummy and the chimp would turn upside down and look at the bull. That was what he was known for." Womack was a rodeo hero of his time, and an inspiration for his lively young daughter.

After six years on the road, Womack came back to Phoenix to restart the construction business he had left when he and Karen's mother had separated. Karen and her mom and siblings had stayed on the property,

Karen Performing Her Trademark Shoulderstand on Tootsie With The Flying Cimarrons

sixty-six acres of commercial citrus grove plus the barn. Her mother had remarried, though, and Karen couldn't stand her foul-mouthed stepfather; she usually was able to distract herself from his behavior by throwing herself into her riding.

Karen's Introduction to Rodeo

Until he returned to Phoenix, Andy Womack didn't realize how serious his daughter had become about trick riding; she had even joined a saddle club for which she trick-rode and showed. Once he understood, he became a big booster. "One of the highlights of my teenage years," Karen remembers, "is that I got to trick ride at the Phoenix Rodeo when I was fourteen. That was a real special thing for me, to get to work with my dad at the same rodeo. He helped me practice. He'd go get on his mule and he'd coach me and tell me what I was doing." She already knew a few tricks, but she hadn't had the kind of in-depth critique that her father provided. Not only did he get her that job, he helped her obtain her Professional Rodeo Cowboy Association (PRCA) card, which she needed to work in professional rodeos.

Karen's dad engaged his hero, the world champion trick rider Dick Griffith, to come to Arizona to teach his talented young daughter how to do the full shoulder stand. That trick became Karen's trademark as a performer. In a full shoulder stand, you have to dive over the horse, upside down. "Most trick riders today do not do a full shoulder stand," says Karen. "They will do a side shoulder stand. A full shoulder stand is hard. I tried to learn to do it before I took lessons from Dick, and I used to just run that horn through me all the time. I put a rubber ball on the horn, but I never did know how to dive into it, and when I went to take lessons from him, I was eighteen years old. I remember he asked me if I wasn't going to do strap tricks any more and I said, 'No sir.' 'You came up here to learn groundwork?' 'Yes sir.' So he got his pocketknife out and cut all the straps off my saddle. Well, this was like, Yikes! you don't do that! These are leather straps that cost money. And he said to me, 'Now you'll have to learn.' And that was his way. As he said, you can't cheat in the full shoulder stand. You simply have to dive right over the horn. So I learned it because of my dad, because that's what he wanted me to learn, and I loved him so much that I would do anything for him. I would always do it every rodeo I ever worked because of that in a tribute to my dad."

Despite Karen's unhappiness at home, she was well-liked by both her peers and her teachers and she was active in school activities. She had the lead role in an eighth-grade play and later reigned as queen over the annual Thanksgiving Day football game. In her senior year of high school she was voted "most popular" girl and elected to the National Honor Society. She became friends with some of her teachers and attracted many peer friends. As a young woman of nineteen, she was even elected as Miss Rodeo Arizona in 1958 and was the first First Lady of Rodeo in Arizona.

Andy Womack hoped his daughter would grow out of horses after her turbulent teenage years, but she never did. In college she was offered an opportunity to apprentice for Rodeo Ben, a Western clothing designer who made elaborate costumes for rodeo stars. Her home economics major would have made her an ideal candidate for that job, but she was so smitten with rodeo and trick riding that after a year and a half she quit college and married a rodeo man. "I got married because I wanted to rodeo," she confides, "and my dad, even though he did not raise me, was very strict about not wanting me to date cowboys, or to be around them, because at that time it was a much rougher world. Everybody portrayed the rodeo cowboys as drinking, fighting, cussing. And he just didn't think it was proper for a young single girl to go down that road. I thought, 'Okay, I should marry the first person that asks me,' so that I could be properly married so I could go rodeo. The marriage didn't work out, but I do have a lovely daughter from that relationship."

So, Karen joined the rodeo, despite her father's warnings. In those days, rodeo committees were usually haphazard about hiring trick riders, and the results were often less than interesting for audiences. Later, the committees started hiring "contract acts" — performers who worked together and put on creative, choreographed shows.

Newly divorced, still in her twenties and with a young child in tow, Karen formed a group with three others, one woman and two men. They called themselves the Flying Cimarrons; "cimarron" means wild and unruly. They played rodeos for a few years, and after they split up, Karen and another member, Dick Hammond, teamed up with Dick's wife and brother-in-law to form the Fireballs. Rodeo committees loved their acts and they got lots of gigs.

Karen Was Devoted to Her Dad

Karen adored her father, but they butted heads too. Back when she was a high school senior, she was living with him when he decided to move to Yuma, Arizona. She refused to go with him because she didn't want to leave her friends and school right before graduation. Angrily he told her she could go back to live with her mother, which he knew she would never do. Instead, she lived with an aunt while she finished high school.

She was active in a lot of activities and knew she'd get awards at graduation; always wanting to impress her dad, she deeply wished he'd come to watch her graduate. Her guidance counselor suggested she just keep writing letters to her dad to let him know what she was doing, even though he wouldn't speak to her because he was so angry at her for not accompanying him to Yuma. Seems that her keeping in touch finally got to him, as he did attend her graduation and said "I always raised you to be independent, but I never thought you'd use the independence against me."

Despite his earlier reservations and his absence from her life during her childhood, Karen's father became her biggest supporter. He kept tabs on her; wherever she performed, she would get a letter from him, sometimes to her surprise. Toward the end of his life, though, she once again unwittingly provoked his ire. He was eighty-one at the time and organizing an Old-Timer's Rodeo in Phoenix. By then Karen was happily married to Harry Vold. Her dad had called Harry and asked him to send their notorious bull, Crooked Nose, to the rodeo. Crooked Nose had lost a horn when he was young, bashing it into a barrel and went on to become the most feared bull of his era. With Crooked Nose on the bill, the Old-Timer's Rodeo would be sensational, her dad must have believed.

As the day of the event approached, the organizer called Karen to express his concern that her elderly dad intended to go up against Crooked Nose. He knew that even as a young man, the celebrated Andy Womack wouldn't have outwitted this bull. Karen told the organizer to use her as an excuse if he had to, so the man told her dad that Karen wouldn't allow him in the arena with Crooked Nose. For an entire year he refused to speak to her, without ever telling her why.

When he was dying a few years later, at the age of eighty-five, she was able to spend his last days with him. When she was told he was dying, Karen was at a rodeo in Odessa, Texas. She immediately made arrangements to be at his bedside, and he, in typical fashion, knew just where she was supposed to be: in Odessa. His birthday had just passed, so when she arrived, she said, "Everybody decided to get together and get you a birthday present and they sent me." Perhaps this was her way of explaining her sudden visit, without directly addressing his dying. She knew he wanted to die at home, so she arranged for him to be released from the hospital.

"He was a very generous person, and you could never outgive him," she says now. "No matter what you did, he always wanted to do something ten times more for you. So I never felt like I could ever do anything for him that was as worthwhile as those last five days I spent with him. We had long talks, but more important I was able to do for him what he couldn't do anymore for himself. I got him out of that hospital.

Karen Found Her Soul-Mate Through Trick Riding

As a young woman, Karen and the Fireballs traveled a great deal, even to rodeos in western Canada. That was where Karen met her future husband, the stock contractor Harry Vold, who had hired the Fireballs to come up to Canada and work for him all summer. The two started a relationship, about which Karen was uncomfortable because Harry, a good fifteen years older than she, was a married man with four children. He invited them back a second summer, unheard of in the rodeo business, lest he lose his connection with the young, attractive, and talented trick rider. Eventually, Harry moved down to the States and started buying up rodeo businesses.

Canadian law was strict about divorce, so it was eight years before they were able to get married. When the law changed, Harry's youngest daughter excitedly called Karen, to tell her that at last the couple would be able to marry. Karen was thirty-three.

After her marriage, Karen retired from the trick-riding circuit to raise their combined family and run the stock business with her husband. These days she trains trick riders with her partner, Linda Scholtz; they run several well-attended clinics each year. Their trick-riding school, which takes place over several weeks each spring, is eagerly awaited by young people around the country and as far away as Belgium. A few years ago the Volds built a large indoor arena to ensure that no freak snowstorm could cancel the course, as had occurred more than once, even in southern Colorado.

Even though Karen did not raise Harry's children, she grew to love all of them. They built a Brady Bunch combined family, one child of hers, four of his, and one of theirs as a couple. The family members are intimately connected, not just because of their love for one another, but because all are related to the rodeo business in some way. Some, like daughter Kirsten, are in business with their dad.

"I never thought I'd have a silver wedding anniversary," Karen says, "but that's come and gone, so that's doing good when you've had such a late start. We've had a very good working relationship and a good marriage, and we're blessed with one child of our own. Kirsten probably was the cement, the glue, for bringing us all closer together as a family. She has a unique relationship with each one of her brothers and sisters. Different, but she always got along well with each one of them individually, and yet much younger than all of them. She was more than twelve years younger than my oldest daughter, and that's the closest one, and then the rest are much older than she is. We are blessed that way, because the kids all are very respectful of their father. They would do anything to help him, and they're all involved in the rodeo business, which is unusual to start with, in a family that large."

Karen & Harry At Colorado Springs Rodeo, 1998

Rodeo people are continually on the road, so Karen's family members don't see much of each other during the year. When they meet, it's less likely to be in each other's homes and more likely at a rodeo in a distant state. So they often gather for Christmas at the National Finals Rodeo in Las Vegas. It's not exactly a conventional family life, but Karen loves it. "Probably one of the best things about the rodeo business," she says, "are the people that you meet. There's a lot of hardships, lots of ups and downs. Long miles, short sleep, short nights, long days, bad weather, cold weather, hot weather. You'll probably experience in one summer what most people do in five years. You do a lot of living in a short time. But it's the people that you meet and enjoy. It is a unique occupation."

Daughter Kirsten, who now runs the Vold stock business, "eats, sleeps, and breathes" the business, just like her dad did. Karen compares both to the Pied Piper: they attract people to them wherever they go.

The Family Vold's Stock Horse Business

The whole family is dedicated to the well-being of their precious horses. Some animal-rights activists complain that the rodeo business injures horses by forcing them to perform unnatural acts. But that couldn't be further from the truth, says Karen. Their livelihood depends on the horses, so they are well cared-for. "A bucking horse has the desire to want to buck like a racehorse has the desire to want to run," Karen explains. "And if they don't have that desire and the heart to want to buck, you're not going to make them buck. People that don't understand think that the strap that you put around the flanks makes them buck. It does *not* make them buck. All that gives is a signal." At most a bucking horse bucks a total of sixteen seconds in his workweek, and that's if he's a very good bucker and performs at a big rodeo.

The bucking horse is like any performer, Karen points out. When the curtain opens and the music starts, that is the signal for the performer to begin to entertain. When the cowboy uses the flank strap, he's telling the horse that it's time to buck. Trainers choose horses that want to buck, then coach them from youngsters. The next stage is the rookie riding competition, which exposes the young horses to coming out of a chute gate, an experience that can be frightening at first. But soon they learn what is expected when the rider pulls on the flank strap. After their performance, the flank strap comes off. That's their signal to stop. Their job is over for the day.

"My husband likes some of the old horses that buck every time," Karen says. "They are the old performers, the 'campaigners' as he calls them. They know when you open that chute gate, that's their cue. This particular horse named Satin was getting old, so we thought we'd be doing him a favor by not taking him to Cheyenne. When they went to load up the other horses, he was just loose and the guy that was loading them had to get him off the trailer three different times. When he'd go get another horse, Satin would be standing in the way, and they'd kick him off. And he just kept wanting to be going with us. The next day he had a heart attack in his stall. Didn't struggle, didn't do anything, just died, but I have always felt that he died of a broken heart, because he didn't get to go."

Karen Feels Blessed by Her Life in Rodeo

Karen was inducted into the National Cowgirl Hall of Fame in 1978. She was booked for rodeo performances right before and after the induction ceremony; she was so rushed that she didn't even have a cowboy hat. She was inducted the same year as her childhood heroine, Tad Lucas. Lucas was charming and gracious and tried to ease Karen's embarrassment for lacking the all-important hat. "If I ever have the opportunity to make amends," she said, she'd be sure to be properly outfitted. While at the Cowboy Hall of Fame to receive the Tad Lucas Memorial Award, she kept her promise, wearing not only a cowboy hat, but full Western dress.

Being inducted into the Cowgirl Hall of Fame was more than Karen ever anticipated for herself. She is full of gratitude for the life she's had and can't begin to count all the highlights: riding as one of two color guards in the parade for Jimmy Dean in Houston, Texas; presenting the American flag at rodeo openings for thirty-three years; going to Helsinki, Finland for her birthday in 1991, where they put on a Wild West show in the Olympic Stadium; holding the first trick-riding school in Maui, Hawaii; celebrating her fiftieth birthday with a "This Is Your Life" party celebration put on by her kids and attended by friends from all over the country.

None of this would have happened, she believes, if she had not gone into rodeo — even though she had to buck her father's advice to do it. If she hadn't become a trick rider, she would never have met her beloved Harry. Now almost seventy, Karen no longer does trick riding herself, but she loves teaching, and watching her students perform. "You feel everything that they feel," she says. "You see everything. When they miss something, you just feel it all because you live it with them. So that's a good substitute: if you can't do it yourself, you coach."

Karen's Spirituality

She doesn't think about regrets, although as a devout Christian she came to feel abashed about all the bitterness she had carried for decades toward her stepfather. She went to find him at the end of his life, made amends to him, and that lifted a burden from her.

As a girl, Karen was head of her church youth group and went to Bible camp. The minister asked campers to step into the circle if they wanted to serve the Lord. She very much wanted to, but couldn't because she knew she wanted to be in rodeo, and how could one serve the Lord in rodeo? Later she learned that "I can serve with my actions. My life can be an example to others by trick riding if I conduct my life in the proper way and as a child I didn't understand that."

Thirty five years ago, hospitalized after surgery for a breast cancer scare, that turned out to be benign, she was suffering from old back injuries incurred while trick riding. She was forced to lie on her back, and the pain became intense. In desperation, she took pain medication. It gave her the dry heaves, making her even more miserable. Alone, not wanting to worry her family if it didn't turn out to be a malignancy, she talked to God. She told him that she regretted taking those pain pills and that if he would relieve her of her back pain, she would never take pain medication again. After a fitful sleep, she woke up without pain. From this time on, Jesus became very real to her. Her favorite scripture verse is Philippians 4:13: "I can do all things through Christ." She and her partner, Linda Scholz, who is also a religious Christian, now run what they consider to be a ministry, in the way they conduct their trick riding clinics. This is one of many ways she "steps into the circle to serve the Lord."

Rodeo culture has changed a good deal since Karen was a young girl, when cowboys were rough and vulgar. The Fellowship of Christian Cowboys has taken hold; now church services are held at most rodeos and cowboy ministers are common. Christianity and rodeo, two powerful forces in her life, are no longer pulling Karen in opposite directions. This is a welcome change for this woman for whom religion has been such a potent influence in keeping her sane.

When I met Karen, she was recovering from an accident that had dislocated her shoulder months before. In her teens and twenties, she had several accidents while performing risky horse stunts, but she has managed to remain agile and active well into middle age. Then she was blindsided by a colicky horse that she was trying to comfort. In his distress he kicked her and threw her up in the air, injuring her shoulder and her kidney. She endured many months of restricted movement — a considerable trial to a woman who thrives on physical activity and does plenty of it while running the ranch. "I have very strong faith," she said at the time, "and I really believe that there is a reason, all things work together for good. I just haven't quite figured it out yet, why I was supposed to be slowed down.

Karen says, "I have great perseverance, a no-quit philosophy, which can verge into stubbornness ... a short fuse," she says, compared to her Mr. Nice Guy husband; Harry doesn't lose his cool, and he does what it takes to get along with people. She's more willing to stick her neck out, particularly when it comes to defending her brood, whether it's children or horses. Then she takes action and "can fight like a banty rooster" to protect their best interests.

Sharon Camarillo

Barrel Racing Trainer & Former Champion

As we walk life's trails, we each have had the chance to experience our share of challenges and celebrations... Life is a learning opportunity and for us who choose to survive, it truly is a great life!

—From Sharon's acceptance speech when inducted into the Nat'l Cowgirl Museum & Hall of Fame in 2006

When you watch Sharon teaching in her training videos, *Barrel Racing: Simple Strategies for Success* and *Ride the West: Barrel Racing Clinic*, you will see her riding her student's beautifully muscled grey mare, Jewels. She has a mic pinned to her Western shirt and looks the part in her cowboy hat and tailored jeans. She tells us exactly what she is doing and thinking about in the carefully designed skill drills she puts every horse and rider through. In her mid-fifties when the videos were filmed, she rarely is out of breath, even loping around and around the arena while she is narrating instruction for her audience.

Even though Sharon won championships at a young age because she was fearless and just went as fast as she could, she didn't become a student of equestrian learning until she decided to educate herself at the late age of thirty. Now she is dedicated to creating responsive horses and educated riders for a safe, enjoyable ride that requires knowledge and training in the basics. So, in the training videos she has produced, Sharon takes the viewer back to the basics, echoing the classical riding disciplines, even though she rides with Western tack and a loose rein.

Sharon Prepares Horses for the Barrel Pattern

First, Sharon trains her horses with ground work in a round pen using side reins, which help them to gradually get used to the feel of the bit. When they are no longer intimidated by the bit, she helps them to get their poll up above their withers by using first one side rein, then two, then tightening them so their head and poll are just where she wants them to be, while still riding with forward motion. She teaches the horse how to rebalance himself and get his impulsion coming from the rear. When she completes the ground work with a horse, he is familiar with self-carriage. Only then does she proceed to mount a rider.

She teaches students by isolating five zones of the horse: 1) nose to neck, controlled by the reins, 2) shoulder, controlled by reins and impulsion from leg aids, 3) rib cage which is balanced laterally with the leg, 4) the hip, where the leg behind the cinch encourages the horse to travel in a straight line, and 5) the hind end, where the impulsion needs to originate. In directing the horse through a barrel course, she teaches her students how to use all of these zones in precise ways.

She describes the barrel course work using the acronym, ART, standing

Sharon Turning Barrels

for Approach, Rate, and Turn. The approach requires a method of steering the horse from the start point and consistently directing him to what is called the "pocket" in barrel racing. Sharon describes the pocket as the "turning area between horse and barrel." In order to be able to leave the barrel from a close distance, he must be positioned within the pocket.

During training, Sharon places visual landmarks – she uses cones — to help the rider and horse identify the correct distance from each barrel within which to approach the "pocket." She places the cones around each barrel to remind the rider of the exact place to signal the horse. At the first (or 2nd) cone, depending on the horse's ability, the rider asks the horse to "rate," or shorten the stride, for the turn.

The "rate" involves sitting, moving the point of contact in the saddle to the back of your jeans' pockets, which shortens the stride, using leg pressure and then rein pressure so the horse can manage the turn in a balanced way. She places the cones further from or closer to the barrels, depending on how experienced the horse is; the more expert – the closer to the barrel. In either case, the horse needs to finish the turn close to the barrel in order to be in position to travel straight and balanced to the next barrel.

The rider looks to the pocket point of the next barrel, requests rate at or between the 1st and 2nd cone, picks up the inside rein to signal the turn and rides to the 3rd cone. For practice, she asks the horse to do the pattern in both directions. The turn is always "prepared, planned, and productive." The rider needs to pick up the outside rein to keep the horse from losing his shoulder.

The horse must be trained to be supple and flexible to create an "arc," the bending from nose, through poll, shoulder, and loin. The inside hock reaches up and across the outside hock. In the turn, the horse is precisely placed in and around each barrel.

In training a horse on the barrel pattern, Sharon starts him at a trot. It's only much later that she introduces the lope, then the speed that enthusiastic audiences are accustomed to seeing in a barrel racing competition, as the riders gallop at full speed from going round one barrel to approaching the next barrel.

Since barrel racing is a timed sport, in order to do it safely both for horse and rider, it requires forward motion, being on the correct lead, the ability to stop and rate (shorten stride), holding the direct and indirect arc in a turn, riding in a straight line, and rapidly changing direction, stopping, and backing up. The horse must be supple and flexible, both laterally and longitudinally. Very different from the way Sharon barrel raced as a young competitor, when it was go fast and faster still and perhaps change the bridle to get more response from her horse.

The Suburban Cowgirl

Sharon, the future nationally known trainer, coach, and TV commentator, grew up in the Los Angeles suburb of Redondo Beach in the 1950s. Her family's modest house was three miles from the ocean. "I thought it must have been huge," she says now, "but thinking back, remembering the location of the dinette and breakfast room and how we had to drop a leaf after we ate so we could walk through the kitchen — it must have been tiny. But it was always organized and decorated."

Sharon's family fit the *Father Knows Best* stereotype of the era. Her father, Bob Meffan, commuted to Northrup Aviation, where he worked as an aeronautical engineer. Her mother, Avril Meffan, tended the home and children. But Sharon's mother had an adventuresome streak. As a young woman in her early twenties, she had made her way to California from the Midwest; she worked before her marriage and had her own car. Once married, though, she embraced the role of a postwar wife and mother. She sewed all of her own and her children's clothing, frugally saved her quarters for treats for Sharon and her younger brother and kept the house in perfect order. Nevertheless, Sharon sensed that her mother was not entirely satisfied, and she grew up determined not to succumb to the traditional woman's role as housewife and mother. However, Sharon always respected her mother's graciousness, her way of making a home appealing, and her commitment to putting her family's needs before her own. She tried hard to build those qualities into her own life as a married woman, a celebrity rodeo performer, and a trainer.

Sharon's parents scrimped to take their children on camping vacations in beautiful, remote sites in the western United States. From the beginning Sharon felt more at home in the country than she did in her suburban town. She was introduced to horses by her father, who took her for pony rides every Saturday as a three- or four-year-old. She loved riding on top of a big moving animal. But it was her mother who introduced Sharon, then a preteen, to Jack Pole and his daughter, Wendy, the connection that marked the beginning of her serious involvement with horses.

Pole had a livestock auctioneering business in San Jacinto, California. Sharon and Wendy became constant companions: they shared a passion for horses and the outdoors. As teenagers they worked together in the livestock business on weekends and during the summers. On Saturdays, sale day, she and Wendy would bring the cattle up into the sales ring, working on horseback — not that anything on horseback felt like work. During summer vacation, they would accompany Wendy's father to pick up cattle and bring them to the sale location. Sharon was fascinated by the livestock business. For a while she wanted to be a cattle auctioneer, even though there were no female cattle auctioneers at the time. The two teenage cowgirls loved wearing jeans and getting dirty. They even raised a couple of colts.

When Sharon was fifteen, her dad took her and the Pole family to the prestigious National Finals Rodeo when it was in Los Angeles. Sharon bought a special Western outfit for the occasion, a white Levi jacket and jeans. At the rodeo she saw barrel racing for the first time and knew immediately: "This is what I want to do." The idea of riding as fast as possible around barrels captured the heart of this athletic, well-coordinated, competitive girl. When they got home, she and Wendy put trash cans up in the field and practiced barrel racing.

Sharon was hooked on the Western lifestyle, Western garb, the animals and their smells, and the outdoor life in general. This prompted some fierce arguments at home. Her father supported her teenage apprenticeship in the livestock auctioneering business, but he objected to his daughter's insistence on wearing jeans in their suburban neighborhood.

When Sharon was a teenager, the voices of women's liberation were just beginning to be heard. Options were opening up for young women that their parents hadn't imagined. Sharon's dad hadn't bargained for a feisty and passionate daughter who had her own not exactly traditional agenda. He recommended secretarial school; she didn't want to go. But she did find a way to follow her own passions and satisfy her parents' wishes at the same time. She agreed to dress in a more feminine way when she wasn't around horses. "I will present myself as a lady," she decided. "I will be proud of my education. I will work on my articulation. I will also work on my equestrian skills and I'll be the best at both. It's allowed me to stand out amongst my peers. So, I appreciate my dad's patience and input."

The tension of earlier years seems to be completely dissipated as Sharon is now close with her dad; at age eighty-eight, he lives an hour away from her in northern California and has traveled around the world with her and her son, Wade, several times each year. Her mother, Avril, died not long before I met Sharon in 2004.

Sharon received a rodeo scholarship to Pierce Junior College in 1966. To accommodate her family's prescriptions and her own fervent desires, she started at this agriculturally-oriented community college in San Fernando Valley, studying dairy and beef production science. She took secretarial courses along with agricultural ones so that she'd have a marketable skill when she graduated. "I gave my dad a little of what he wanted in order to achieve what I wanted." she explains now. The college had an intercollegiate rodeo team where she could participate in events like roping and goat tying.

Then she was granted a scholarship to California State Polytechnic University, the agricultural and engineering university at San Luis Obispo, where she earned a bachelor's degree in agricultural business and economics. To cap her college career, Sharon was the first runner-up in the Miss College Rodeo pageant, honored for her poise, appearance, and horsemanship.

When Sharon graduated from college, she was offered opportunities that would have led to professional positions in teaching or television, but she opted instead to become an airline stewardess — considered a glamorous job for women in those days. She was more certain than ever that she wanted to become proficient in barrel racing, the only women's event in professional rodeo. She bought a horse and started training it for rodeo. Her schedule as a stewardess for Western Airlines allowed her to train horses and ride in rodeos.

Bitter-Sweet Romance With a Cowboy

In 1974, when she was twenty-seven, she met her future husband, Leo Camarillo. She was impressed with his credentials: Professional Rodeo Cowboy's Association Team Roping Champion for four different years and the association's All-Around Champion yet another year. Sharon was flattered by the attention of a real-life cowboy. Even though their backgrounds couldn't have been more different — Leo came from a family of Mexican migrant farm-workers — she was determined to tame this "diamond in the rough." "Leo came from a different religious background," she says. "He came from a different educational background. He came from a different value background. It was tough. But it was wonderful. I wouldn't have been the individual I am today, with the strength of character, the ability to rebound, resilient in the public's perceptions of me, if I hadn't met Leo."

Sharon was determined not to relinquish her independence in the way she believed her mother had done. Since both she and her husband were strong-willed, they often clashed. In the 1970s, Sharon and Leo created and ran Rafter C Productions, which manufactured and sold roper supplies. The two competitors maintained a busy travel schedule for twelve years. During the winters they followed the rodeo circuit in Texas and Arizona, then they returned to their home in northern California, where she ran the roping business and managed the 150 acres of grassland that they leased out. "It was a 70/30 effort," she explains, "I felt we needed to take advantage of Leo's industry recognition to build a rodeo-related business, combining my college degree in business." But Leo was traveling the circuit most of the time, while she stuck closer to home to run the business and competed in regional competitions.

She qualified four times for the National Finals Rodeo and was the Women's Professional Rodeo Champion, riding her husband's horse, Charlie, and a horse that she trained herself, called Seven. "In barrel racing," she explained, "the horse is a big part of it. You've got to manage him and train him, lay the foundation. When you have the exceptional horse, it is like the exceptional individual. You can educate a horse. You can buy his breeding. You can buy his conformation. You can train him. But he has to have the heart to excel, to be great. I had that horse. My husband said, 'You have a horse that'll make you a world's champion.'"

But at that point, Sharon decided to retire from professional competition. She was pregnant at the time, and after her son, Wade, was born, it became clear that Leo not only didn't know how to be a father, he wasn't interested in learning. Sharon was taking care of an infant and running the family business pretty much on her own. Pursuing the world champion barrel racer title was no longer her priority.

The things that are and always had been important to Sharon were "home, security, holidays, grandparents, traditions and education." She tried to maintain these during her marriage, even when Leo didn't want to participate. She didn't believe that traveling on the circuit with a young child at home was the best environment for Wade; when she did travel, she took him with her as much as possible – he developed a wanderlust from all his world travels — and her parents were generous in staying home with him when necessary.

When she became a mother, Sharon realized she was ready for a new challenge – being on the circuit didn't intrigue her as much as it had in her twenties. "Motherhood changes even the most driven individuals, always for the better... I chose my profession and loved the competition; however I wanted to work toward something more stable and permanent... I have never looked back on my decision to retire from professional competition. All good things come to an end and timing is everything ... Learning from challenges and being prepared to move forward are traits that I continue to cultivate."

In retrospect, Sharon notes that being a celebrity in the rodeo world as Leo was made it difficult for him to remember that life doesn't revolve around him. He was accustomed to women's adulation of his prowess in the arena. Leo didn't take well to sharing the stage with a youngster — or with his determined, independent, and competitive wife. Instead, he sought out women who would give him the uncritical and undemanding adoration he had come to expect.

Sharon Goes Back to the Basics

Despite the success and acclaim, Sharon had hit a professional wall; she realized that she didn't have the equestrian training to be able to evaluate and improve her own performance and those of her horses. Like other barrel racers before her, she had catapulted into stardom and bypassed the basics. In barrel racing, she explains, "all we need is a horse and an entry fee. As a young girl I had a ranch horse and three trash barrels, and when the local rodeo came to town, I entered and got to dress up and be a barrel racer." The sport's requirements were straightforward. "One of the reasons I chose timed eventing," she adds, "was that it was not judged, so I didn't have to have the clothes. Couldn't have them anyway. Didn't have to have the fancy horse, didn't have him, couldn't have him, couldn't afford it. So my choice was the timed event. It was exciting. It was fast. And people could be a part of it without any skills. Just that God-given ability to go fast and be fearless was what allowed me to accidentally win."

After a while, winning accidentally wasn't enough. Winning makes some people complacent, but not Sharon; she realized that there was a whole world of equestrian knowledge out there and she wanted to explore it in a disciplined way. Drawing on her own and Leo's connections, she contacted local trainers, including Lindy Burch, the world champion cutter (see Lindy's story) and Bobby Ingersoll from the snaffle bit industry. She started taking reining lessons from Gary Ballmer, who was a regional champion.

She learned about riding on the correct diagonal, how to control the rhythm of the stride, how to make a horse more supple, what to do when your horse is bracing against you. Before, when she hit a snag, it had been "Let's just change bits and go fast again!" Now she was developing an understanding of horse and rider that enabled her to understand the problem and develop a training program to fix it. The more she learned, the more she got excited about coming back to barrel racing with a plan based on serious training and understanding the needs of the individual horse and rider.

Sharon has come to believe that making a plan is key; she makes short-range, mid-range, and long-range goals for herself. She told an interviewer: "It's important that goals are realistic, believable, and achievable. To set them, you need to determine your weaknesses, recognize your strengths, and seek solutions ... Goals are important because they keep you disciplined, focused, and in a positive direction."

Sharon also began collaborating with her old college roommate, Sharon Gill, from the Gill Ranch, an old ranch holding in Fresno, California. When her friend went to events that required her to do reining, cutting, pattern work, and roping, Sharon did one of her friend's events. "So I made my barrel horses into reining cow-horses, "Sharon says, "fed them down, softened them up, got them in the bridle, and experimented with the judged event, reining cow-horse. I was never top level, but it gave me wonderful skills to then sort out and bring back" to barrel racing.

She realized that barrel racing horses are not often "cross-trained" in other disciplines; consequently, they react instinctively to the barrel pattern, but are often uncontrollable outside of the arena. That no longer appealed to her. In contrast reined cow-horses are trained to be all around ranch, roping and cattle horses; they're trained to do maneuvers in front of a panel of judges. Not so with barrel racing horses; they merely have to beat the clock, not with any particular form or finesse. Exposed to her friend's horses and the competition she entered, she got inspired to cross-train her horses. "It helps a horse to be more consistent in a broader variety of conditions... I enjoy riding a horse that responds to the rider. When my money is on the line, I want to help the horse make winning decisions."

Sharon Begins Teaching Students

These skills also laid the foundation for Sharon's subsequent success as a teacher. Now Sharon maintains a busy schedule giving barrel-racing clinics all over the country. In the past twenty-five years, she has trained more than 10,000 students, ranging in age from preteen into the sixties. She continually challenges her teaching and her horsemanship; she asks herself:

is my presentation well organized? How could I have gotten through to my students more effectively? She's never stopped asking and improving her teaching and consultation. She thinks of herself as a life-long learner, a "work in progress."

To enhance her teaching, Sharon has published instructional videos and two books, *Barrel Racing Training, Tuning, and Winning!* and *The A.R.T. of Barrel Racing*. She also produces two Sharon Camarillo Classics every year, one in Sterling, Illinois and the other in Reno, Nevada, where her barrel-racing students can showcase their horsemanship. The motto for the Classics is "Look for the star in you."

She is an enthusiastic teacher and counselor to her students, caring about their welfare and how they make decisions about their lives, as well as about their horsemanship. "Horses are just an extension of relationships we have in life," she says. "There's a reward system. When we're correct with them, they return to us. When we're inconsistent with them, they're inconsistent with us. We put a lot of pressure on our horses. We bring them into our lives for entertainment, for support, for friendship. We forget they're animals that need training. It's like training a child and using patience. Patience is the process of retraining or repeating the education."

Over and over again she encourages her students to look at the big picture. "Don't just look at somebody because they won first place and think they're going to be the total answer," she urges them. "I want you to see how they treat their horses at their home. I want you to see how they act with other horses. I want you to see how consistent they are. Use your common sense and judgment in selecting a mentor. I think that works in friendship. You don't like a friend because they dress well. You want to see how they act in different environments, how they treat their family."

Nothing makes her happier than knowing that she's having a major impact on her students' lives. As an example, she shares this note from one of them:

"When I went to your first clinic, I was ready to give up. I was in real need of one person giving me some solid consistent advice. I had a million people telling what to do and how to do everything and the novice barrel racer I was I just got confused and disgusted. And what I learned from your first clinic I just took it and ran with it, it was what I need to keep on trying."

Media Celebrity

Sharon's talent for informing and educating has found another outlet in the mass media. With the legendary rodeo announcer Bob Tallman, she co-hosts the successful cable television program *Spur of the Moment*. She also hosts *Ride the West*, a series on Horse TV.

It was Bob Tallman who got Sharon into television. In 1992, he introduced her to David Glodt, the TV producer, who asked her to be the female commentator for the Houston Livestock Show, the largest stock rodeo show in the world. She was thrilled; she loved the show and attended whenever she could. As a novice commentator, Sharon was sometimes frustrated because she wasn't as articulate as she wanted to be. More experienced mentors advised her: "Don't memorize your opening. Just get the concept and talk." Now, when the camera comes on, she knows exactly how she's going to begin, and after that the words just flow. She's come to enjoy her commentating role.

Now she does the College National Finals Rodeo and other horse-related programs for cable stations. "That gives me a chance to wear the nice Western clothes I like to wear," she says, smiling broadly. "I think I do what I do because I like to dress Western. This gives me a venue to wear the lifestyle clothing I tried to convince my dad was part of my life." These days she doesn't have to convince her dad of anything – he's proud of her, whatever she wears.

She is working on a project for RFD TV, called *Fun and Fast Times Hosted by Sharon Camarillo*. She is also working on a new book for Lyons Press called *101 Tips for Better Barrel Racing*. She produced *A Rider's Resource Guide*, which she gives to each student who participates in the Performance Horsemanship Clinic.

Tad Lucas and Other Awards

In 1997 Sharon was honored with the Tad Lucas Award by the National Cowboy Hall of Fame and Western Heritage Center Museum in Oklahoma City. Tad Lucas was a champion cowgirl and trick rider of the 1930s and 1940s. Each year the award is given in her memory to a woman who embodies Lucas's spirit of achievement in the field of rodeo and Western horsemanship. The award committee selects women who display excellence in business as well as performance in and out of the arena; it is meant to honor those whom it believes "uphold and promote our great Western heritage," according to the website. It's one of the few ways that the Cowboy Hall of Fame recognizes women.

Because Sharon respects the role of equipment in horsemanship, she has thought long and carefully about what kind of reins, what kind of saddle, what training equipment is best suited to the barrel racing industry, Sharon has collaborated with manufacturers, such as Reinsman Bit Company, Ariat Boots, and Courts Saddlery, that distribute her line of Western tack and gear. She was recognized by the Western and English Manufacturers Association in 2004 for her contributions to Western design and then again in 2006 by WESA with the Top Hand Award.

Sharon's Family Life Turns Sour

During the years that Sharon was becoming so spectacularly successful as a horsewoman, instructor, commentator, and entrepreneur, her personal life was falling apart. Her husband, Leo, she finally admitted to herself, was having affairs; he became both physically and mentally abusive. Finally, after twenty-eight years of marriage, many of them troubled, Sharon divorced him. "The divorce was very tough for me and my son to go through," Sharon says. "I had fought for the total family unit. Food on the table. I can have it all. Be a good wife and mother and a professional." But Leo was unable or unwilling to do his part.

Sharon is both realistic and resilient. Once she acknowledged the enormity of the chasm in her marriage, she began to make the independent decisions that built a stable life for Wade and for herself. "One of my mantras is, like I tell my son, the best revenge is a life well-planned and well-executed," she says now. "Don't let another person knock you down. I have to believe all of these things come into your life for a specific reason, to build me into the person I am supposed to be. That at the end of my life, I feel like I'm ready to move on wherever that next step takes me."

Sharon attributes her resiliency to her strong spiritual beliefs. As a girl, she often visited her grandmother and great-aunts in Missouri, where her ancestors settled. While there she went to church with them regularly, absorbing the Southern Baptist teachings they believed in.

Another of Sharon's personal challenges has been to parent her teenage son, Wade. She has conscientiously searched for the best way to nurture him. When he was a youngster, he struggled in school with academics and with social relationships. Sharon would spend hours at his school to support him and the teachers and to help him develop into the best person he could be. After the marital separation, Wade, witness to some of the violence at home, wanted nothing to do with his famous father. Neither did he want anything to do with horses. As a youngster, though, he was smitten with cattle and helped his mother run the farm. After trying college for a year, Wade joined the Navy; he's an Aviation Boatswain, stationed on the aircraft carrier, U.S.S. John C. Stennis, in Bremerton, Washington, hoping to make a career out of the Navy. Sharon is proud of his choice and his persistence in following through on this career decision.

But, Wade has his social side as well. He consistently accompanied his mother and grandfather on trips all over the country, as well as some international travel. For Sharon who is instinctively shy in public, Wade acted as a welcome buffer on their trips.

Sharon has learned from experience that the choices one makes early on become the consequences and rewards of tomorrow. She urges her young students to "milk your parents for everything they're worth — stay at home and get your education. Be prepared." Supporting oneself emotionally and spiritually is crucial, so she surrounds herself with people who believe in her, those from whom she draws energy and whom she admires. She leads a public life in many ways, but she guards her privacy at the same time. Her inner circle is not large. She wants to have time to reciprocate the love her close friends give her. Part of her remains shy and even self-effacing. "I'm embarrassed when it comes to someone adoring or complimenting me," she admits. "I feel like I do the best I can. I learn from every mistake that I can. I'm a work in progress and my success just validates what I'm doing."

Getting married again isn't high on Sharon's priority list. "I really believe that if God thinks I should have a male around, it'll fall into place one way or another," she says. "He'll have to be quite persistent. Very understanding. I wouldn't be easy to live with. I've run my life, my way, too long." It's a life full of good friends, challenging work, horses — and more. Although she loves the horse world, she does not "live it and breathe it," as some horsewomen do. Instead, she cultivates her interest in the arts, music, collecting Western memorabilia, and interior design. She likes to create and market Western clothing.

Her home is her sanctuary. Its décor reflects the places she loves; its warm saffron color invokes the Tuscan countryside she is so fond of; the floors are tiled with gold Saltillo pavers in appreciation of the big Texas ranches. Her Victorian-style bedroom features heavy dark brown and burgundy brocades and lace, with antique silver brushes and vintage pictures of cowgirls. "I admire the early ranch women," says Sharon. "They were gutsy. They fought outside the box. Not only did they raise a family and put food on the table, but they were outside beside the men trying to eke out a living from a tough environment."

Women Who Have Inspired Her

In addition to the old-time Western women, such as Annie Oakley, Sharon has been inspired by modern women who have what she calls "the heart of a cowboy and presence of a lady." These women are effective in the public sphere and nurturing in the private, family sphere. One of her close friends is Reba McIntyre, the country music singer, who sang her first National Anthem at Sharon's first National Finals Rodeo. Reba, says Sharon, is like a helium balloon, "the higher, the farther, the better for Reba."

Sharon's best friend, Jimmie Gibbs Munroe, world's champion barrel racer, has a ranch heritage from the Wild West show background. As president of the Women's Professional Rodeo Association, Munroe was instrumental in bringing recognition and equal earnings to women in the professional rodeo world. She ran a successful cattle-buying business. "I admired the quiet graceful way Jimmie Munroe does business," Sharon says now, describing what drew her to her friend. "I admired how she rode and trained her horses. I admired her pre- and post-actions as a competitor. I incorporated those skills into my program."

Another friend, Dot Abbott, became blind after a minor car accident, when an airbag severed her optical nerves. She still runs her home as if she had her eyesight.

Through the daunting challenges of her adult years, Sharon Camarillo managed to maintain her dignity and integrity, her determination to improve and excel. But she embraces her life now, every day of it, cherishing the time with her son, her father, and her dear friends, her students and work associates, and the time she gets to spend alone in the home that she decorated in just the way she likes. She relishes the diversity of her horse-related work and looks to the future when she can add even more skills to her already full life.

Sally Swift

Creator of Centered Riding

The very act of trying brings tension and rigidity; the horse responds to our stress with his stress, and the downward spiral begins ... Sally Swift, with quiet wisdom and gentle understanding, asks us to reassess our habitual responses and in so doing alter the way we approach riding and training horses.

Edward Emerson, Jr., President., U.S. Combined Training Association, From the Foreword to Sally's first book

Few equestrians, male or female, have truly transformed our understanding of the horse-human relationship. The late Sarah Rodman Swift, known as "Sally Swift," creator of Centered Riding, was one of the few. Sally passed away on April 2, 2009, just before her 96th birthday. *Centered Riding*, the first of the two books that introduced her approach, has sold more than 800,000 copies in fifteen languages. In a survey of German equestrians who were asked to name the top one hundred people worldwide who had influenced their riding, Sally Swift was number four, one of the few women and even fewer Americans to make the list. At age ninety-five she received the seventh annual Equine Industry Vision Award from the Pfizer Animal Health and American Horse Publications for her visionary methods that have enhanced riders' experience in all disciplines.

Sally's Visionary Centered Riding Approach

What made Sally Swift's approach so revolutionary when she published her first book in 1985? Sally introduced the idea of using one's body in the most effective way to relieve stress on both the horse and rider; since horses are such exquisitely sensitive creatures, they respond best to clear messages that are free of tension. Centered Riding incorporates martial arts, awareness of how the body and mind affect the horse's behavior, knowledge of human and horse anatomy, and creative visualization processes, all with the goal of encouraging the harmonious partnership of horse and rider. Sally's methods are applicable to equestrians in all disciplines, from beginners through world-class competitors and to horses trained at any level.

As Sally described it in *Centered Riding 2: Further Explorations* (2002), the method "is a way of re-educating the mind and body toward greater balance and integration ... A centered, balanced rider with good awareness of her body and that of her horse can help her horse develop correct musculature and move with balance and freedom of motion. The horse has a chance to work in harmony with his rider and take pleasure in his work rather than develop stress, and all too often, pain. This freedom of motion leads to efficiency of movement, which in itself produces beauty."

Centered Riding rests on "The Four Basics": soft eyes, diaphragmatic breathing, centering, and the building blocks. What do these concepts mean? "Soft Eyes" allows the rider a greater field of vision, increased awareness of her own and her horse's body, less tension, and easier, more free forward movement. Diaphragmatic Breathing, taught in yoga and martial arts, also reduces tension in the rider's body, helps to lower her center of gravity and thus allows the horse to become quieter and more responsive while reducing rider fatigue. Centering encourages the rider to find her center of control and energy deep in the lower body, releasing tensions that block the flow of energy. This promotes a more stable and secure seat. By thinking of her body as a series of Building Blocks, the rider is able to achieve a true and consistent balance over her horse's center of gravity.

Centered Riding Training

Students of Centered Riding, whether they are recreational riders or instructors-in-training, start on the ground — off the horse — in order to develop an awareness of their own bodies. In the Open Clinics, open to any level rider, students are asked to think of the parts of their body as children's building blocks and to softly stack one above the other in this way: at the bottom are the legs and feet; above them is the pelvis, then the ribcage and the shoulders, and finally, the neck and head.

To help the student visualize how her body should be aligned, Sally used vivid imagery; "imagine a bungee cord being pulled straight up out of the top of your head ... pulling you up like a puppet and feel the upward surge of energy through your whole body ... Imagine you are a giraffe with a graceful curve of the neck, instead of a turtle that has difficulty extending its neck." As William Steinkraus, Olympic gold medalist in show jumping, noted in his back-cover endorsement of her first book, Sally Swift's approach is "wonderfully imaginative in finding just the right psychological images to help go beyond the mere mechanics of riding."

During groundwork, students often work in pairs, with one playing the horse and the other the rider. By mirroring each other's movements, they learn to mirror the movements of the horse. One exercise Sally introduced to teach mirroring is "Dancing Hands," which is based on t'ai chi ch'uan, a martial art that focuses attention on body awareness, the breath, and the balanced body. It goes like this: one student is the leader and one the follower. They touch the palms of their right hands together. The leader moves her hand and arm and her partner follows every movement, as if the two hands were joined by a strong magnet. The students' feet remain in place, but all the joints above can move. If either partner stiffens, communication between the "dancing hands" is blocked.

Other such exercises on the ground demonstrate how an almost imperceptible movement of the bit is felt by the horse; one person, the "rider" holds the reins just the way she would when mounted, while the other, the "horse" holds onto the other side of the reins. When the rider barely begins to close her ring finger on the rein, the human "horse" is aware of the pressure. When the person who is role playing the rider stands behind the "horse," and directs the horse with the slightest touch on the ribcage, she can affect the "horse's" movement. These kinds of simulations give students body and mind training for what the horse experiences. Since horses are even more physically attuned than most humans, presumably the most subtle movement or pressure is registered.

After students have done these ground exercises, they experiment with what they have learned to see how their actions affect the horse. The instructor performs bodywork to help each student find her "center," that place deep inside a rider's body that gives her a "quiet strength, harmony and power." Students might work mounted, using a longe line with eyes closed to experience the movement of the horse and to "go with" that movement. The instructor directs the students through a series of exercises that introduces them to the key concepts of Centered Riding, including the Four Basics described above.

Part of Sally Swift's acclaim likely is because her diagrams and visualizations give people such a clear sense of how to achieve a balanced and following seat, so necessary for the comfort of horse and rider. As one reviewer of her books wrote, Centered Riding instruction "bridges the gap between left brain and right brain" knowledge. Right brain training gives the rider the experience of deepening the seat, relaxing all one's muscle groups, and an awareness of what it feels like to "go with the horse."

Sally Gravitated to Mind-Body Techniques from Her Own Disability

Sally lived in a small shingled house that she bought in 1966, situated on a quiet side street in Brattleboro, Vermont. "I intend to live here till I die," she declared. She almost had her wish; weeks before her death, she was moved to a nearby nursing home with a bout of pneumonia. She died with Centered Riding friends, who were her "family," and her devoted caregivers, including her dear friend and protégée, Lucile Bump, gathered around her.

At the time of our first interview, Sally sat at the kitchen table in her favorite straight-backed chair, enthusiastic to tell her story once again. She was humble and warm, attributes she demonstrated to anyone who ventured through her life. Her followers describe her as a person who could relate to people of all types, despite having had an upper-class upbringing and having garnered recognition world-wide for her teachings.

She presented herself as articulate, laughing heartily at her recollections, and thoroughly enjoying telling her story. She had the broad vowels and clipped speech of an educated, well-bred New England woman. Her mind was active. She remembered details of events from decades ago even though she complained of forgetting where she put things yesterday. When she got up from her chair, she moved slowly, using a walker, a testimony to her age and the scoliosis that propelled her to pursue horseback riding as a youngster in order to give each side of her body equal exercise. Her living room housed a treadmill, which she still used, but only when her caretaker was there. "I'm very cautious," she told me. She attributed her longevity to her health-conscious attitude – healthy eating and exercise. When I visited Sally a few years later and only months before she passed away, she had become more reliant on her round-the-clock caretakers, but she still was capable of waxing enthusiastic about horses and riding.

How did Sally Swift evolve into a woman with such sensitivity to horse and human? Sally was born in 1913 in the seaside town of Hingham, Massachusetts. She was proud of her family background and liked to talk about their accomplishments. Her father, Rodman "Tod" Swift, came from a wealthy New Bedford family that had made its fortune in whaling and commercial shipping. Sally was instrumental in getting the book *Sea Struck*, published in 2004 by W. H. Bunting. The book draws heavily on the clandestine log that Tod Swift kept during his year as an ordinary seaman. When his daughters were young, he had tried to interest Sally and her older sister, Agnes, in the joys of sailing. Agnes took to the water and became a proficient sailor, but Sally was intrigued with horses from a young age.

When she was small, the garbage man used to collect trash with a horse and cart. At the age of two or three, she was allowed to sit on the horse's back in front of her sister, while the horse pulled the dump wagon. She remembers loving the smell of the horses and their breath as far back as that experience.

As a little girl, Sally took walks with her mother and spent "blissful" hours gazing at these big, graceful creatures. When she was ten, her family rented a horse for her and her sister for a month in the summer. Helen KingBolt was an old carriage horse; Sally and Agnes would alternate taking walks on her down a quiet country road, under their mother's watchful eye. "We always timed it so we wouldn't get mixed up with the trolley car," Sally recalls. "We had it wrong one day and we were walking toward home and the trolley came up behind us. It had no mercy and went 'ding, ding, ding.' Didn't slow up or anything. If Agnes had been on the horse, goodness knows what would have happened. But Helen would never take a wrong step as long as I was on her. These horses take care of you."

When Sally was eight, she was diagnosed with scoliosis, lateral curvature of the spine, possibly caused by undiagnosed polio. Her mother took her to the famous Miss Mabel Ellsworth Todd of Boston, a practitioner who nowadays might be called an occupational therapist; she practiced a method something like the Alexander Technique. The Alexander Technique teaches how to change simple everyday habits of movement to improve balance and coordination by releasing unnecessary tension.

In those days, recounts Sally, she was irritable and prone to temper tantrums; one day, she even kicked her mother — and felt guilty afterwards. Mabel Todd advised her mother, "Don't scold her for it — you just have to let her have a tantrum and get it out of her system ... It's part of her life caused by the tension the curvature puts on her body." Fortunately, her mother listened to everything Todd advised and was very patient with her daughter. She once wrote a paper on Centered Riding titled "How Having Scoliosis Led Me to Centered Riding." She wrote, "My remarkable mother did all this without ever making me feel like I was queer or different. She made nothing of it ... We didn't dwell on the fact that I was different. She did a good job, and it has stood with me all my life."

Mabel Todd may have devoted herself to Sally's care because they shared some commonalities. As a child Todd suffered from an illness that severely weakened her kidneys. A bright student, she developed a passion for science, guided by an exceptional science teacher. Later she injured her back in a serious fall. While recuperating, she used her understanding of high school physics and anatomy to try simple movements to strengthen her body. At the late age of twenty-six, she went to Emerson College of Oratory; there she studied the interaction between movement and voice.

Before long Todd was developing a private practice, where she applied what she had learned while healing herself to healing other people with disabilities. She would work with patients on the treatment table, where she used pictures of a skeleton to illustrate ideal body balance; then she would ask her patient to modify their movements, based on the ideal balance noted on the skeleton. Later when Sally developed her Centered Riding methods, she used a model of a skeleton to demonstrate how the body of the human and horse are constructed and how they move with and without tension.

Todd constructed fanciful metaphors and directed her students to focus on the image while she touched the exact location of the problem in the body. Students were to practice these images while they walked, rolled over, or crawled. She was one of the pioneers in developing a body-mind connection, one that Sally also incorporated into her Centered Riding philosophy.

Todd began writing about her work concerning ideal body alignment from a mechanical perspective in 1920. Her ideas engendered a following, and soon the director of the physical education department at Columbia, Dr. Jesse Feiring Williams, offered her a B.S. degree; because of her pioneering work, Todd was exempted from many of the required courses. She became a lecturer in the department and later published *The Thinking Body* (1937). This book, which has become a classic and is still in print, is the study of human physiology and the effect of psychological and mental processes, such as visualizing images, on human movement.

Mabel Todd might have instructed Sally to squat down and "walk like a duck." Or she would suggest that Sally visualize "dragging an imaginary alligator's tail along the ground" when she was walking. Her techniques gave Sally the skills she needed to strengthen the muscles in her lower body and to rebalance the uneven muscle tone caused by her scoliosis. Sally owed many of her sensitivities to Miss Mabel Todd's decades-long treatment and nurturing of her.

Miss Todd encouraged Sally's interest in riding; she believed it would strengthen her back muscles and use both sides of the body equally. When Sally was thirteen, Miss Todd instituted a new regime. She decided that Sally had too much strength on her right side, so she must develop her left side. "She made me do everything with my left hand," Sally says, "including writing, brushing my teeth, eating, playing any kind of sport. And generally upset my life totally. She decided I had to do something, so I loved riding and she realized riding was good for me, because it was equal on both sides. So that's what I did." Sally believed that Mabel Todd's work saved her from becoming a cripple; she took private "lessons" with Todd twice weekly until she was in her early twenties.

The Emergence of Centered Riding Concepts

Having been a student of Mabel Todd's for so many years, Sally began to apply her teachings to her work with horses. Gradually she became aware of a place in her pelvis that she thought of as her center of gravity. "My concept at first was that I had a ball in my upper body and when I dropped it into my pelvis, it would land there with a thunk like mud." It gave her a sense of groundedness when she worked with horses.

In her early twenties, when she first started teaching riding, she tried it with her students. She knew that this "centering" had made a difference in her own riding and it seemed to be helping her students, but she didn't feel confident enough to present it as a theory of riding. "You don't want to be out in left field," she said, especially as a young, inexperienced instructor. What would her adult students think if she blurted out, "Imagine a ball dropping into your pelvis with a thunk like mud"?

While a high school student at Milton Academy outside Boston, Sally met the English riding instructor Phyllis Linnington, whose rigorous teaching was Sally's first introduction to real discipline as a horsewoman. She spent most of her junior and senior years at Phyllis's barn; she doesn't remember much about her schoolwork, but she did graduate with honors.

Feeling that inactivity would be hazardous to Sally's back, Mabel Todd did not want her to go to college, so Sally apprenticed herself to Phyllis for the next three years, including one summer in Sussex, England. Phyllis's standards for horse-keeping and conditioning were high, and Sally learned much from her about stable management. All the horses' feet had to be washed before they went out and after they came back to the barn. No rationale was offered; Sally later imagined that Phyllis required this because of all the rain and mud in the English countryside. Horses had to be groomed daily and tack was cleaned each evening. In between grooming and cleaning, Sally exercised the horses. "She was a stickler and a driver, but

I learned a lot from her," Sally said about Phyllis.

Linnington believed that a rider's knees could not be too tight against the horse's sides, so she instructed her students to carry cardboard between their knees and the horse and do one hundred rises without stirrups. Later, Sally had to unlearn this method in order to develop soft knees and ride with relaxed legs.

As an instructor, Phyllis emphasized a balanced seat, similar to what was taught at the Spanish Riding School in Vienna and discussed in former director Alois Podhajsky's classic book, *The Complete Training of Horse and Rider in the Principles of Classical Horsemanship*. Later Sally became a master at creating visuals to convey the concept of the Building Blocks, stacking one part of the body over another, a visual cue for how to achieve the balanced seat that Phyllis Linnington taught.

After her apprenticeship with Phyllis, Sally taught and schooled horses at the Boots and Saddles Riding School in lower Manhattan. The School was run by Colonel Guirey, a Russian Cossack prince, a cultured person and a "real gentleman." He was so quiet and unassuming that at first Sally mistook him for just another instructor. She was stunned to find that what she had practiced so long and hard with Phyllis was deemed incorrect by Colonel Guirey. Having learned to clamp her knees hard against the saddle flaps, she now had to soften them — by riding the sitting trot with stirrups for fifteen minutes at a time. "If you didn't have soft knees, you'd die at the end of fifteen minutes," Sally remembered. Her knees, she said, "have been soft ever since." She rode much better after that because when your knees are soft, you are better able to follow the horse. Rather than perching on top of the horse, you become part of the horse's movement.

Colonel Guirey was a gentleman in an environment where not every man could be called that. In Sally's youth, riding was often taught by professional grooms, who could be gruff and yell at students. Colonel Guirey was, in marked contrast, a highly educated and refined man. Sally used Guirey's style as a model for her own teaching.

At the riding club, Sally was able to try out some of her methods on adult riders. One of the horses she rode there was Kim, a high-strung Standardbred who jigged incessantly and never walked. Sally tried all the tricks she knew to calm him and get him to walk. Nothing worked. At last Sally merely breathed calmly. Kim settled right down and did a flat-footed walk.

Sally was flabbergasted. She tried breathing and then not breathing. Kim had felt Sally's relaxed state and responded in kind. Sally began teaching breath-work to her students. She was among the first to recognize how responsive horses are to the internal state of their riders. This and other techniques that Sally experimented with as a young instructor are well accepted today, but in the first half of the twentieth century they were new. Sally Swift was ahead of her time.

College and Post-Graduate Employment with Cows

After teaching riding for twelve years, Sally realized that she was not earning enough to put away money for her future. Also, she did not want to become a "hardboiled spinster" or one of the ill-mannered grooms, the only role models she had been exposed to in the horse world. Molly Punderson, her friend and former English teacher (who later married Norman Rockwell), persuaded her to go to college, despite her initial resistance to the idea. She started at Massachusetts State College (which later became the University of Massachusetts at Amherst) in 1943 when she was thirty, and then transferred to Cornell University, where she majored in agriculture, with a concentration in dairy farming. She worked as a consultant for various dairy farms, analyzing the milk production of different types of cows.

Then one of her former Cornell professors approached her with the idea of directing the Dairy Herd Improvement Association, a regulatory position. Sally said to him, "Men don't like to be policed by a woman," and he responded, "Not by any woman." In her early forties, she was hired by the American Holstein Association and worked there for twenty-one years. It was this job that prompted her move to southern Vermont, which she happily made her home to the end of her long life.

Sally handled the correspondence for the Holstein Association's testing programs. She was the one who dealt with the farmers, who often didn't understand what the programs were for or why they were important. "I could speak their language, so I was pretty useful to the association." she says. During this time she continued to ride and teach riding for her own pleasure, all the while experimenting with the methods that developed into Centered Riding.

Centered Riding Evolves Further as Sally Gets Help for her Scoliosis

When Sally reached her fifties, her back was giving her trouble again. In 1967 she started working with Jean Gibson, who did the kind of physical therapy that Mabel Todd had done with Sally decades before. Since Gibson was in England, Sally saw her only a few times a year for intensive work, but this was enough to alleviate her pain and make her stronger and more mobile; it allowed her many more years of riding and teaching. Gibson also underscored the importance of "building blocks" — the idea that each part of the body should be balanced on the one beneath it. Sally realized that Gibson's work had important applications for horseback riders.

Sally's experience with disability honed her sensitivity to how the body works. It helped her to be exquisitely attuned to how to achieve balance and harmony in her system and it gave her a strong incentive to pay attention to what her body was telling her; if she didn't, discomfort or injury would result.

In the early 1980s, before her first book was published, Sally studied Alexander Technique with Peter Payne, who also had a martial arts background. One of the exercises she learned from Payne was to look intently at a picture on the wall. Then he directed her to use her peripheral vision to widen her field of vision, while still looking at the picture. This is what she came to call "soft eyes," and it evolved into one of the Four Basics of Centered Riding. "If you get concentrated on things, you get tied into it and hold your breath," she explained. With soft eyes one sees more than what is right in front of one's nose. With Payne's help, she was finally able to shed the hot and uncomfortable back brace she had had to wear all of her life while riding.

In 1975, Sally was sixty-two; after two decades with the Holstein Association, she decided it was time to retire. She had been experimenting with a methodology of teaching riding, derived from a combination of many Aha! moments she had experienced in all of her attempts to strengthen and heal her own body. While in Denver with a friend she saw a book called *The Centered Skier* by Denise McCluggage. The book featured an intriguing graphic: a person with the sun right in the middle of her body. Sally was struck by how similar the concepts and diagrams were to what she had been teaching her riding students. She phoned the author and asked if she could use the term "Centered Riding;" McCluggage agreed instantly.

Germinating Sally's First Book and the Success That Accrued From Her New Visibility

While teaching friends and friends' friends in her lessons, she also audited clinics given by prominent clinicians from Europe and the US. Priscilla Endicott, who wrote *Taking Up the Reins*, a memoir of the year Endicott took in Germany to study dressage, invited Sally to join some prominent instructors at her home. At the time, Sally could not ride herself because of her back, but she was compulsive about attending all of Priscilla's riding salons. She discussed her ideas with the luminaries at Priscilla's clinics, including Denny Emerson, who was reserve rider on the U.S. Olympic eventing team in 1976. Both Denny and Priscilla encouraged her to write about her philosophy. In 1980 she finally began to write her first book.

Coming from a literary family, Sally gravitated toward synthesizing and articulating ideas. She is proud of her heritage and wonders whether the legacy of her maternal grandmother, Mary Halleck Foote (1837-1938), for example, contributes to her being able to use visualization so well in her writing and teaching.

An upper-class New Yorker by birth, grandmother Foote went to the American West with her mining engineer husband in the late 1800s. While there, she began to write and publish stories about the "wild West" mining communities and illustrate books for famous writers such as Louisa May Alcott. She did this all under her own name, rather than taking a man's name as a *nom de plume*. Unusual for her day, Sally's grandmother was a role model for independent thought and action.

Putting her thoughts into book form was a natural progression for Sally. When her first book, *Centered Riding*, was published in 1985, it became a best-seller throughout the equestrian world. Her clinics became even more popular, and not only because she was still charging only $50 for a day's clinic and $10 for a private lesson. She thought she was making good money. She never advertised; her methods spread by word of mouth. A friend, Betsy Hestnes, a well-connected equitation teacher in western Massachusetts, used to hire her to run clinics for her students. Betsy was impressed and told everyone. She predicted that Sally would go far and wide to teach her methods. She was right. By 1983, Sally was asked to teach in Canada; by 1985, in Denver, by 1986, in California and Oregon; to Australia in 1988 and Europe in 1989. Before long, her clinics drew more attention than what Sally could accommodate on her own.

Although Sally had few role models, she learned a lot in later years about horses from Francois Lemaire de Ruffieu, a classical trainer originally from France. A son of a cavalry officer, he also was a member of the mounted cavalry and the famous Cadre Noir. Sally had strong convictions about how to use the body for the best effect on the horse, but Francois added a new dimension of knowledge about horsemanship.

Centered Riding Training

Today there are two levels of Centered riding clinics available to the layperson, from Open clinics for any rider to Advanced clinics to deepen understanding of CR. They both involve ground work – off the horse —in the morning, where instructors train students about their own anatomy and awareness of their bodies' movement. In the afternoon, they ride and put their learning into practice.

Instructor training is rigorous and it takes time to absorb the methods and concepts. After the first three-day clinic, aspiring Level I instructors take a four-day clinic within 4-8 weeks, during which time they practice and assimilate the concepts. Then they do practice teaching with a supervisor, and if they pass, they become certified at Level I. At this level they are allowed to advertise that they use Centered Riding techniques in their teaching.

After at least two years of Level I teaching experience and two update clinics, they are given the opportunity to advance to Level II, which gives them the right to give Centered Riding lectures and demonstrations. At Level III, they can finally offer clinics to the public. Those who reach Level IV have completed an apprenticeship with a Senior Instructor. When they complete the other Level IV requirements, they are the ones who train new Centered Riding instructors, a task that Sally and her associates take very seriously. Level IVs must be both proficient riders and excellent teachers. Quite a rigorous training program.

In 1997, Sally received the Lifetime Achievement Award from the American Riding Instructor Certification program. Her second book, *Centered Riding: Further Explorations*, came out in 2002, when Sally was almost ninety, and was published in nine languages, selling over 100,000 copies. In 2006, Sally was inducted into the United States Dressage Foundation Hall of Fame. In 2008 she was honored with the seventh annual Equine Industry Vision Award, presented by the Pfizer Animal Health and American Horse Publications, an award that recognizes "innovation, ingenuity and service across the entire equine market," according to the obituary on the Centered Riding website. She was pleased to be strong enough to be able to travel to receive this award.

When she died in 2009, Sally had outlived most of her contemporaries and all of her family — sister Agnes died in 2004, at the age of ninety-six — but she remained vibrant and active as the spokesperson and an inspiration for Centered Riding programs all over the world until the end of her life. This kept her in touch with many young people who were devoted to her, and probably helped her maintain her youthful attitude. Former and new students who visited her were surprised that Sally Swift was humble and chatty, still in awe of her own continuing acclaim, never having expected to influence so many horse people all over the world.

Lucy Bump: Sally's Dear Friend and Protégée

If I can teach and ride better and be honest about it,
then I think that I'll get the business.

Lucile (whom everyone calls "Lucy,") started learning dressage and show jumping with Sally Swift when she was fourteen, fifty-plus years ago,

Lucy On Right, Overseeing A Centered Riding Training

and way before Sally became famous for her Centered Riding philosophy of teaching and riding. Even though Lucy had taken some riding lessons at camp when she was younger, her relationship with Sally inspired her to make a career out of horsemanship.

Appropriately enough, Lucy met Sally for the first time at a horse show. Sally had come with a friend of Lucy's father and they discovered, small world style, that Sally's sister, Agnes, had been the librarian at Lucy's grammar school, the Shady Hill School in Cambridge, Massachusetts, where the family lived when Lucy was a youngster.

Having trained with Sally and having hosted her trainings for years, Lucy became a certified Level IV Centered Riding instructor. She maintains a busy schedule, training CR instructors in Europe and South America as well as the United States and Canada. She has taken her Centered Riding training and applied it to her knowledge of other riding disciplines, a practice that fulfills Sally's intent.

Lucy's Childhood With Horses

Lucy began her riding career on the New England dirt roads near what is now Southmowing Stables: A Center for Centered Riding, the facility she started in 1972. Her parents encouraged her passion for horses and horsemanship, but, like many of the women whose stories are in this book, this wasn't an interest that anyone in her family shared; she would have to pursue it on her own.

Her first horse, Majorette, gave her hours of pleasure. As youngsters, Lucy and her friend Dorothy Mount used to ride long distances, up to twenty miles a day, just for fun. She'd ride seven miles to meet up with Dorothy in Halifax Center, Vermont. They'd ride together for hours, then Lucy would ride the seven miles back home. On her return trip, she was sometimes so fatigued that she catnapped on her horse, who knew just the route to get her safely home. Lucy's mother finally laid down the law; Lucy could only ride every other day, "or I'd kill my horse," her mother warned. The two girls were so smitten with riding and showing their horses that they rode to horse shows miles away. Horse trailers were rare in those days.

College and Beyond

While a student at Marlboro College, a small liberal arts school in southern Vermont, Lucy continued to hone her skills as a horsewoman. During the summers, she also trained with Doris Eddy, another of Sally Swift's protégées and one of Lucy's role models. Lucy taught riding at West River Lodge in Brookline, Vermont, and at Camp Renoia in Maine. "I was offered the jobs, so I took them," she says. As she sees it, she stumbled into this business because of luck and serendipity, not necessarily because of her own talents as an instructor.

After college, Lucy went to California to train with Linda Tellington-Jones, before Linda developed the TTouch method (see Linda's story). Linda and her then husband, Wentworth Tellington, were conducting a rigorous training program for instructors at the Pacific Coast Equestrian Research Farm and School of Horsemanship. It was there that Lucy was introduced to all three components of eventing — dressage, stadium jumping, and cross-country — and increased her capacity for endurance riding, already familiar from her childhood riding days. Unlike many horsewomen, Lucy believes in becoming proficient in all different kinds of riding. She has competed in endurance, Western pleasure, combined driving, eventing, and hunt seat equitation.

Lucy at SouthMowing

I interviewed Lucy in her comfortable hundred-plus-year-old Victorian farmhouse just off a dirt road in southern Vermont. She bought this property on her own thirty years ago and put all the work into refurbishing it with the help of young horse lovers who have shared her home with her. The barn was once cow stanchions, filled with junk, some of which still decorates the barn and house. She built and rebuilt the stalls herself.

Before our talk, Lucy proudly introduced me to many of her beloved horses, most of whom she bred herself. "This is Black Rose, dam of White Velvet, Barak, Excaleber and Black Velvet. She is the sister of Black Russian," she told me, very much the mother of them all. She's partial to Lipizzans, the famous white horses that are used at the Spanish Riding School in Vienna; in addition to the Lipizzans, she also breeds Thoroughbreds.

She had already managed the stable at West River Lodge in Brookline, Vermont when she purchased the old property, so she had some confidence in her ability to manage horses and people, but it's always been challenging to meet the responsibility for paying the bills as well. She also discovered that setting limits with people was harder than setting limits with horses. She had some disappointments with people she hired to do work at the barn, but learned from her experiences, realizing "you have to accept people for who they are."

Making a living entirely by operating an equestrian facility was not possible right away. In the early years, she volunteered and sometimes got paid for working on ski patrol, as she had as a college student. For twenty years she worked at night as a paramedic for the Rescue Squad in Brattleboro, then rode and gave lessons during the day. Making a lot of money has never been Lucy's primary objective. Her goal has always been to maintain a safe, comfortable facility for horses and people. "Yeah, there's the business management," she acknowledges, "but if you work hard at the riding and the horses, the other will come along. Maybe that's not the business way to look at it, but there's a certain integrity to that. If I can teach and ride better and be honest about it, then I think that I'll get the business."

Her mentors, Sally Swift, Doris Eddy, and Linda Tellington-Jones, showed Lucy how to get along in the horse business. "I thought they had these things they offered to me and I could take from them," Lucy says. "Like they offered me a plate and you're eating, and you say, 'OK, I'll take this piece and that piece.' I don't have to take the whole plate. You make it your own."

In the peak season, Lucy used to teach as many as ten lessons per day at Southmowing, when she wasn't abroad teaching Centered Riding clinics for instructors who are working toward their next level of certification. Her training schedule has taken her to Germany, Austria, Denmark, and Italy in the summer and fall; when she is home, she travels to various clinics in New England. The income from teaching helps cover the costs of running Southmowing Stables.

Now in her sixties, Lucy extends hospitality to young people from various countries who live in her big house and take care of the horses, as well as give some lessons. She has finally decided that they can do more of the physical labor on the farm, labor that she's done for the past thirty years — but she's still carrying her share of the workload. Every time I've seen her, she's been trying out the new snow blower or bringing horses to or from their paddocks or giving lessons. She does let the young people get on the green horses first, something she always used to do herself.

Looking back at her career thus far, Lucy says, "I wish I had had more of a goal. I didn't know where I was going. Didn't have a plan. The choices were because there was reasonably little resistance and I could do this. 'That's fine, I'll do it,' instead of 'This is what I want.'"

"Clear intent" is one of the fundamental principles of Centered Riding. I asked Lucy what she might have done differently if her intent had been clearer. "I would have worked more on my riding," she replies. "Most of the time was taken up teaching and managing ... I didn't just coast along on the waves," she adds. "I had to push and I had to work hard ... I think if I'd been really clear, I'd have taken more time under instruction. If I knew twenty years ago what I know now, it'd be wonderful. With every horse, you wish you knew a whole lot more when you started them. If I'd been more focused, well, maybe I'd have made the Olympic team. Who knows? But I wasn't."

And the rewards for her hard work have been considerable, high among them the opportunity to work day in, day out with horses, an occupation that she loves. "The horse gives you energy," Lucy says. "They refresh you. And there is the thrill of riding, the 'being one with the horse.' They are also sensitive and require that of you. I like the feeling of riding when the horse comes together under me, whether it is an incredibly balanced horse galloping down a hill in the hunt field or a canter pirouette that my mare Little V does with the lightest of aids. These are the things we look for and treasure ... where the horse is using himself so well that I have all this incredible power with the lightest of aids. This takes training and balance and a lot of riding to get there."

Lucy believes that a key to her success as a horsewoman is mutual respect — her respect for the horses and theirs for her. "Horses should not be walking on top of you. They need to respect you as you respect them. One of the things I say is that the horse and rider thing is a partnership, but you're the senior partner. You need to let that partner do his job, but you're the one that sets the policy. Don't micromanage him."

Lucy's Passion for Foxhunting

For the last twenty years or so, a highlight of Lucy's fall season has been foxhunting with the Guilford Hounds. It all started when a neighbor, Robert Anderson, approached her for riding lessons. After he had acquired some proficiency, he explained that he wanted to ride in order to foxhunt. Then he met a woman who bred a good line of hounds for foxhunting; eventually he took over the hounds and served as Master of the Guilford Hounds from 1989 to 2003. Thanks to her former student, Lucy herself became a passionate foxhunter. For years she never missed a hunt unless she was abroad teaching.

The Guilford Hounds run a "drag hunt," which means that the pretend "fox" (who are really Jon Tobey and his daughter, Katie, who have been doing this task for years) lays a scent early in the morning across farmland that the club has permission to use. The hounds, experienced ones joined by young ones, follow the scent. How well they manage depends in part on the weather; many hunts have been derailed because the wind has dispersed the scent before the hounds have a chance to sniff it. A drag hunt is generally more predictable, and thus safer for hounds, horses, and riders, than a "live hunt" — one in which the hounds pursue a live fox. Because the route is known in advance, the Master of the Hunt can control the hunt's speed and direction. The hounds are not going to be following a fox across a busy road or crawling under a fence that the horses can't jump.

For years Lucy was a "whipper-in" for the Guilford Hounds. This means she would ride up front with the hounds to make sure they are following the scent and not chasing someone's cat or dog. Recently, she retired from this job and now occasionally acts as Field Master, organizing the hunt when the Master is not available.

The allure of the hunt is to watch the hounds work while enjoying the great outdoors, galloping across beautiful country. Newcomers can come and pay for the day, a practice called "capping." Those who haven't hunted before, both young horses and novice riders, start in the "second field," which is somewhat behind the main action and where the pace is more likely to be a trot, not a gallop. The more proficient riders in the first field try to stay as close to the hounds as possible — but not so close that they interfere with the huntsman, which is a big taboo. A good hunter is a quiet, sane horse that can gallop in a group of unfamiliar horses with occasional little hounds yapping at his feet and not get overly excited. A horse that wins blue ribbons as a horse-show hunter may not have the temperament to succeed in the field.

The hunt season culminates in the Master of Foxhounds Ball at the Copley Plaza, an elegant old hotel in Boston, where Lucy and her foxhunting friends get dressed to the hilt and enjoy dinner and dancing.

Lucy recently attended to Sally Swift, when Sally was dying after a bout of pneumonia and Lucy was with her daily until the end. With no children of their own, I wonder if the two women felt like family, family they could choose.

Anne Kursinski

Olympic Show Jumper & Trainer

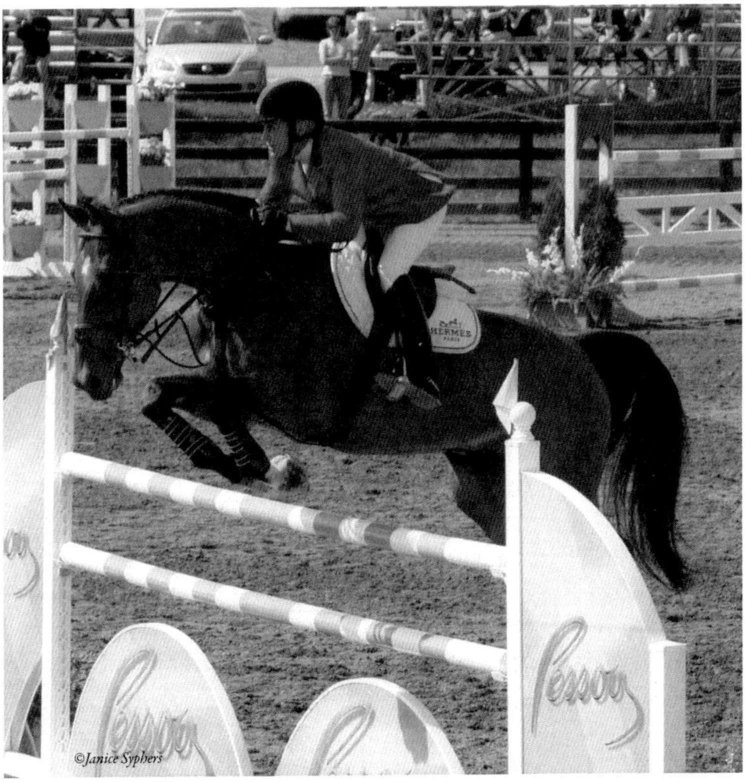

©Janice Syphers

Anne on Great Point, 2006 Sussex County Grand Prix

I'm passionate about what I do, my riding and teaching ... keeping the horses fit and healthy ... From all that, the winning comes.

Anne's Early Introduction to Equestrian Activities

Anne Kursinski, trainer and four-time Olympic show jumping competitor, started her equestrian career early, thanks to her mother, Mary Jo Kursinski, a dedicated amateur rider who introduced Anne to horses while she took lessons herself. Anne was all of four years old when she started riding at the Flintridge Riding Club in La Cañada Flintridge, in the foothills of Southern California's San Gabriel Mountains. Established in 1922, the Flintridge Riding Club had long been known for its high standards. In 1956, seven years before Anne started riding there, the famous horseman, Jimmy A. Williams, had joined the club as its riding master and begun to develop a comprehensive instructional program that became renowned for both its training methods and its eminent graduates — a group that eventually included Anne herself.

Anne remembers being picked up at school as a youngster, butterflies in her stomach in excited anticipation of getting to ride. From the beginning Anne was drawn to "the fun of it, the excitement, dealing with these great big animals and being this little tiny person, being able to control them and get them to do things." Already she was dreaming of becoming a professional rider and trainer. For years, though, she kept her dream secret; only later did she confide in her trainers and her family.

She started jumping on the Flintridge school horses at about age five. Although she took instruction in flat work and dressage with the beginners' instructors three times a week, show jumping quickly became her passion, one from which she never wavered. Every weekend she'd spend as much time at the barn as her mother would allow. She was enthralled. When she wasn't riding or helping out with chores, she could be found intently observing the barn's best riders as they took lessons and schooled their horses. Within a year or two she was competing herself.

Her younger sister, Lisa, also a fine rider, won more ribbons than Anne did, but she didn't have the same passion for horsemanship. As an adult, Lisa still rides and gives lessons. Older brother Robert was never interested in horses. He became, quite literally, Anne explains, a "rocket scientist," who works for NASA's Jet Propulsion Laboratories.

When Anne was eleven she got her first horse, Rice Field, an off-the-track Thoroughbred. Rice Field, an older horse, helped Anne develop her jumping skills. At about this time, Anne's parents separated. Anne's immersion in horse activities helped her get through the family's difficult times. "I'm sure my horses heard all my woes ... They were my saviors, my friends and buddies," she remembers. Like the other student riders, she rode bareback on Flintridge's cross-country course; she bathed her horse and decorated his stall. While her home was confusing and even tumultuous, the barn provided a haven of stability where her place was secure.

Influence of Jimmy Williams

Soon Jimmy Williams noticed Anne's insatiable interest in learning and took her on as a student, catapulting her from the charge of the beginner instructors into the ranks of the favored advanced students. The young Anne knew that being chosen by Jimmy was a momentous opportunity. Jimmy Williams was world-renowned for his success as a horseman and his students likewise set a high standard. Anne was nervous. "I hope I'm good enough that he wants to take me," she recalls thinking.

From the mid-1950s Williams had specialized in hunter-jumpers, but he was a Renaissance man when it came to horsemanship; he knew dressage, racing, polo, and Western riding. He even had been a stunt man in movies that used horses, like *Ben Hur* and *A Day at the Races*. Now he's in the Hall of Fame of the National Reined Cow Horse Association as well as the Show Jumping Hall of Fame. While in the U.S. Army during World War II, he organized races and horse shows in Italy.

"He was a real cowboy, nothing classical about Jimmy," Anne says now. "Yet he read a lot of books and he was a good horseman. He could get inside their heads. He could get them to lie down. To jump on a moving freight car. Jump through a plate glass window."

Jimmy was a huge influence in Anne's younger life. Because she had such a keen desire to succeed, she paid close attention to everything he said. It was a thrill to be chosen to train with him. In the beginning, he gave her some positive feedback and encouragement, but as she got better and began to win ribbons, his trademark abrasiveness surfaced more and more often. Though his criticisms were sometimes demeaning and often caustic enough to hurt, Anne hung in, knowing that not only was Jimmy a master horseman, he was a trainer able to bring out the best in both riders and horses. With his meeker students, he would be generous with his praise, and he'd never put them on the tough horses that might embarrass them by throwing them off. At one point, Anne envied these girls, and wondered if they were being treated better because they were prettier and wore nicer clothes.

But the more potential he saw in a student, the more he demanded — and Anne Kursinski had plenty of potential. What she heard from Jimmy, over and over again, was "You'll never be good enough." He thought that critical and demanding treatment would motivate her to try harder and aim higher. When she "got a little too big for my britches," perhaps after winning a championship, he'd put her on a problem horse that would buck her off. Those difficult horses may have undermined her confidence, but they also taught her a great deal about horsemanship.

Looking back, Anne acknowledges that Jimmy's technique had the desired effect on her—it "made me more tenacious," she says—but at the time his harshness exacerbated her own self-doubt and made her wonder if she were capable of achieving her dream. This is not a method she would ever use with her own students. Later, when Anne had become a world-class show jumper, she heard through others that Jimmy was proud of her—but he never said anything to her.

One of Jimmy's practices made a lasting, positive impression on Anne and prepared her for her later accomplishments as an instructor and trainer; he had his more proficient students give lessons to younger kids. She relished "the mentoring, the power and control of helping someone else, the satisfaction, being able to make changes. Same with horses, to make a difference, get the most out of a horse or student. That all started in my teenage years."

In those days the pinnacle of the U.S. horse world was in the East, where the competition was toughest and where the top riders got their start. When Anne was about seventeen, Jimmy Williams took her and other Flintridge riders to the National Horse Show at New York City's Madison Square Garden. Anne placed in show jumping—a major accomplishment for a young woman from the West. Jimmy, of course, wouldn't let her get cocky; he'd challenge her with a green horse or an ornery one. "That's the humility of working with horses," she says. "You win the Grand Prix one day and then you fall off the next time."

Flintridge and Jimmy Williams opened the doors that enabled her to ride to the top of equestrian competition. In 1976, her senior year of high school, Jimmy took Anne to Spruce Meadows, an important horse show in Calgary, Alberta, Canada, to work with the U.S. Equestrian Team. For the first time she was exposed to big money and big names in the horse business. She saw some of the best riders in the world perform there — and dared to believe that maybe, just maybe, if she worked very hard, she could be one of them.

"As a young girl," Anne says, "I'd sit and look at the picture books of Mary Chapot, Bill Steinkraus, these famous riders. Rome, Aachen, Wiesbaden. Wow! And I hadn't really talked about this Olympic dream when I was little. From California, you'd never go to the Olympics. I didn't think I was so good. And then sure enough, later in 1983, I finally get to go to Rome, the Grand Prix. I got to go to Aachen. I've been to five Olympic Games."

Making a Decision to Pursue Her Equestrian Passion

At the girls' high school she attended, Anne was a B student; her report cards suggested she'd do better if she were more committed to academics, but that was not her passion. Students were expected to go on to college, so it was with trepidation that Anne approached the headmistress, Mrs. Trower, to tell her that after graduation she was going to take a year off to work professionally with horses. To her surprise Mrs. Trower commended her: "You are fortunate you know what you want to do," she told the nervous student. "If this is your passion, go for it." Anne never forgot those words and the support they represented. They helped her believe in herself.

Her father, a schoolteacher as well as a musician and church organist, was disappointed when she decided against going to college. She never exactly decided not to go to college; instead, she thought "I'll take a year off" — and the year went on forever. Now she counsels her young students to go to college and sometimes wonders if she would have had more expertise as a business person had she continued her education. She might have had a little guilt at the time, especially about letting her father down, she confesses, but she was so clear about what she wanted to do, she didn't let these doubts sway her.

Because she started school a year earlier than most, Anne had enough course credits to graduate by the time she was a junior, so she had more time for competing. Her mother, who by then knew of her Olympic dreams, said, "Go for it!" Her father, however, couldn't imagine his teenage daughter sacrificing her higher education in order to compete in horse shows. After the divorce, he often took Anne and her sister and brother to cultural events in Pasadena, like opera and theater. He attended some of her shows but, unlike her mother, wasn't an especially enthusiastic spectator. He came around, though, when she started to win big honors in the show jumping arena and is now her biggest fan; he's even attended the Olympics to watch her compete. Though Anne didn't pursue higher education, she has never stopped learning and challenging herself, and she, like her dad, is a teacher with more international visibility than her father ever dreamed about.

Studying Dressage

In 1976 Jimmy Williams invited Hilda Gurney, Olympic bronze medalist in dressage, to coach Anne and Susie Hutchison, another top young rider at Flintridge and one of Anne's role models. Anne studied classical dressage with Hilda, learning lateral movements, such as shoulder in, leg yield, and half pass, and exercises that supple, strengthen, and prepare the horse to excel at any sport. Under Hilda's tutelage, Anne trained and showed dressage at the Grand Prix level while she continued to work for Jimmy, teaching and schooling horses. Hilda felt certain that Anne could compete at the highest levels. Unlike Jimmy Williams, she made it clear how she felt about Anne's talents and drive.

Hilda became a mentor to Anne, who was inspired by Hilda's story — how she started out with no money and climbed to the Olympics. Hilda's style was the opposite of Jimmy's. "Good correction, honey," she'd tell Anne after she recovered from a mistake. A schoolteacher as well as a horsewoman, Hilda used positive reinforcement in her training, which contributed to Anne's "burning desire" to go professional.

Anne Leaves the Safety of Jimmy's Barn to Join George Morris

In 1981 in her early twenties, Anne left the safety and familiarity of Jimmy's barn, against his advice and without his blessing, to move to the East Coast. She had been schooling between twelve to fifteen of his horses each day, as well as giving lessons at Flintridge, so Jimmy stood to lose a great deal by her leaving. It wasn't easy to gather up her courage to defy Jimmy, who had been such a big presence in her life since she was five years old.

In California, she had already won several Grand Prixs in show jumping and had made a name for herself. Now she'd have to prove herself against some of the greatest athletes in the equestrian world. She was still training with Hilda Gurney, who encouraged her move. "Anne, if you want to become a top dressage rider, and ride for the [U.S. Equestrian] Team, you could follow that dream," Hilda told her. Around that time, she also met Kathy Kusner (see Kathy's chapter), who rode for the team and whom Anne considered "like a God." Kathy was world-renowned in the show jumping world; she had ridden in several Olympics and won medals. She had also transformed the landscape for women who aspired to become race riders by going through a grueling court battle to get the first jockey's license for women. She was clearly a role model for the young California show jumper, and she gave Anne a "Go, girl" blessing to try her stuff in the East.

Anne had known of George Morris, who trained with the legendary Hungarian-born Bertalan de Nemethy (whom Kathy Kusner trained with as well); de Nemethy was one of the world's great dressage and hunter-jumper trainers, as well as the Team coach for the U.S. Olympic show jumping team from 1955 - 1980. Morris, one of his protégées, continued the de Nemethy tradition and became an Olympic competitor. She contacted Morris and he was happy to welcome her to his barn in Gladstone, New Jersey, where the USET trained. Anne ended up working closely with Morris, who became another important mentor. They had a business relationship, but her space in his barn was always separate and he permitted her to build her own clientele there. He was strict, regimented, and authoritarian, a style she knew well from her years with Jimmy, so she acclimated easily. They did well as a team, because Anne was always a "good soldier ... a good team player." She knew how to take direction. Morris was the first person who said, "We have to get you an Olympic horse." She had landed in the right place.

Training Olympic-Level Horses

Morris found Anne her first Olympic-level horse, Livius. She and Livius became a great pair. At twenty-one she was the youngest person to make the U.S. Equestrian Team, as an alternate. She was beginning to live her dream! She and Livius went on to win gold medals first at the Pan Am games in 1983, then at the Grand Prix in Rome.

With George's assistance, she found a succession of Olympic-level horses. Horses who are mentally and physically capable of reaching the top are hard to find and they don't come cheap. But by then Anne, under George's tutelage, had established enough contacts in the horse world to find people willing to buy into a syndicate — finance the purchase of a horse by becoming its part-owners. Many of these people were philanthropists who relished the prestige, the opportunity to show their patriotism, and the thrill of being participants at the Olympic Games. Apart from these glamorous but intangible benefits, investors may be attracted by the potential resale value of an Olympic winner and, to a certain extent (especially for stallions and mares), its value as a breeding animal, although Anne explains that breeding is not as lucrative in the United States as it can be in Europe. At some venues, such as the Grand Prix at Spruce Meadows in Canada or the Global Tour in Europe, hefty financial rewards accrue to the winners.

The people who participated in syndication of Anne's horses, however, did it more to support her and to be part of the glory of sending a horse to the Olympics than to make money from the investment. When Anne solicits investors to join her in buying a potentially great horse, she doesn't try to dazzle them with visions of big profits. "Some people are motivated more by money than I am," she acknowledges. "All these horses could probably have been sold along the way. I could have made a good commission, but that would not fulfill what is in my heart and my desires."

After Livius came Starman, a German horse that she found through horse dealer Astrid Winkler Bolton of Hamburg, Germany and Miami, Florida, another influential woman in Anne's career. Anne still waxes eloquent when describing Starman. He was a "great horse," she says unequivocally; he was courageous, confident, and willing to jump anything she aimed him at. "He put me on the map," she adds. "The bigger the competition, the better he performed." At a smaller show, he might get careless and knock a rail down, but "the bigger the crowd, like at the Olympics, he wasn't intimidated, he would rise to the occasion. He knew it was important. So he was a big part of my life for a long time." She rode him for years and won many honors, including the Grand Prix of Aachen, Germany, in 1991. She was only the second woman and the third American to win this coveted prize.

Starman helped build her confidence as she faced the daunting jump courses of international competition, but then he was injured and had to be retired. For top equestrian professionals there is always the chance that the superb equine athlete who has carried them so far will go lame and need to be replaced.

Soon, Anne found her next horse partner, a five-year-old named Cannonball, again through her friend Astrid Winkler. "He was a bit of a monkey," Anne admits. "He could buck and spook, but he was a very talented horse. I nursed him along in terms of his lack of self-confidence. All the ability in the world. He could jump a house; he was like a little rubber ball. But chicken sometimes."

As the 1992 Olympics approached, Cannonball was still a little green and he lacked international experience, but several veteran show jumpers suffered mishaps that forced them to withdraw from consideration, so Cannonball made the team. In the team event, he and Anne were eliminated because "he stopped out" — refused three fences — and was eliminated. In the second round, in the triple combination (three fences in a row, one or two strides apart), the jumps were huge, between 4'9" and 5'10", and he got scared. The construction was stark and "airy," not "inviting to horses." Anne turned her whip up to "give him more heart, more courage" and miraculously got around the course with only four faults. But Cannonball had never faced such challenges, and, Anne says, "It took his heart away ... he lost his confidence." Witnesses told her she should have received a medal for the feat. "I don't know how I did it," she says now. "I sort of willed it." Nevertheless, Anne realized that Cannonball was not up to the rigors of Grand Prix jumping.

Anne didn't have to search far for her next horse; Eros, a hot chestnut Thoroughbred, was literally right under her nose, boarding in the part of George Morris's barn that she leased. How had she missed him? She'd been on the road, competing in Barcelona and elsewhere; somehow he had escaped her attention. Then, as she and her business and life partner, Carol "Hoffy" Hoffman, were about to leave for Thanksgiving, she watched Adam Wootten, an Australian who had owned and trained Eros, taking him over jumps. Adam told Anne she should try him out. She was intrigued, but her mind was on the impending holiday. Once Thanksgiving was past, she tried him out. She was astonished! He carried his head high in the air, he ran sideways — but he also had a "huge heart," he was "so light off the ground ... more like a deer, he jumped so effortlessly, like a dancer." He was athletic and fearless; he could, and would, jump anything. "He can go to the Olympics," Anne thought. Seven famous riders had tried Eros, it seemed, but none had bought him. "That one was waiting for me," she believes.

Anne rode Eros through Christmas and decided he was a keeper. She found enough investors and bought him. Smart move! Their list of accomplishments is long. "We won a silver medal in the 1996 Olympics and second in the Grand Prix at Aachen," she recounts, cataloguing their achievements. "We won the Grand Prix in Mexico. I was the first woman to do that. He became a very famous horse, earned many accolades. He had the desire to be the best, light and delicate ... Always this delicate dance we'd do together. I'm still riding him, even though he had a bad injury in Florida a year ago. I hope he does compete again if he wants to, and yet he doesn't owe anybody anything. He's still got the spirit. I think he's sound enough to do it." At age twenty-three, Eros is still being ridden four or five days a week; he's still got a great work ethic, Anne says.

Anne and Hoffy Create Market Street Farm

After her long and fruitful association as a protégée of George Morris, Anne decided it was time to strike out on her own. Horse people had long respected her as a trainer and now as an Olympic athlete; her reputation was spreading. After she contributed a couple of training articles to the magazine *Practical Horseman*, a publisher approached her about doing a book. The result, *Anne Kursinski's Riding and Jumping Clinic* (1995), was a collaboration between Anne and another *Practical Horseman* contributor, the writer-photographer Miranda Lorraine. Miranda asked the seemingly naïve questions that coaxed Anne to articulate precisely what she does as a rider and trainer. Sometimes Miranda's questions — how do you do this and why do you do that? — almost drove Anne crazy. But Miranda's persistence as well as her photographs helped make the book better. It solidified her reputation as an instructor-trainer, a part of her work that Anne feels most proud.

In 1999 she and Hoffy bought a property in New Jersey that included an old stone house, but no barn. Together they have transformed it into Market Street Farm, 130 rolling acres in the central part of the state. After so many years under the aegis of Jimmy Williams and then George Morris, it required considerable courage to invest in a large property, build a barn, and to create from scratch a new equestrian business. Hoffy designed and now manages the barn at Market Street, a quiet, pristine place where horses munch contentedly on hay in large, bright stalls. On the walls are photos of Anne and her favorite horse partners from several decades of Olympic show jumping competition. Anne has come to appreciate even more the work that goes into running a top equine facility. The responsibilities are immense, but she and Hoffy have grown into them. "It's the journey, not the destination," she says.

As the owner of a large equestrian facility, Anne focuses on giving back to the horses at least as much as they've given to her. When the horses are content, so is she. "I love listening to the buckets being slammed around by the horses or their nickering or stomping," she says. She learns from her horses by listening carefully for what they are trying to tell her. She relies on animal communicator Marlene Sandler to help her keep on top of what her horses need. She's no longer shy about passing Marlene's insights along to her veterinarian when he's trying to diagnose a problem, even though many people are skeptical about "horse communicators."

One of her supreme goals as a mentor, trainer, and writer is to pass this sensitivity on to her students. She hopes the riders who come to her clinics will absorb the peaceful atmosphere of the barn and observe how the horses are treated. She loves it when students — and, not infrequently, their parents — come back to tell her the impact she has had on their lives and their riding and how she has inspired them not to settle for mediocrity. Olympic eventers Karen and David O'Connor have come to her clinics to brush up on show jumping techniques; eventer Carol Kozlowski (see Carol's story) is another student and fan.

"It's not winning at any cost," Anne emphasizes. When a horse is hurting, some competitors might dull his pain with medication and push him to compete anyway. Anne doesn't work that way. Rather than discard a sick or lame or "problem" horse, she'll nurse him back to health or train him to his highest potential. If a horse can no longer compete at the highest levels, he might be retired or used for less strenuous activities. She is always asking herself, "What can this horse do for me and what can I do for him?" Her winning comes, she believes, as a result of knowing her horses and helping them to excel. This is exactly what she does with her students.

Learning From Horses

She has learned major life lessons from her horses. In the early 1980s, Anne had several concussions after falling on her head, despite wearing protective headgear and a chin strap — something she always did even when many of her colleagues did not. After one of the concussions, she felt dizzy and slow, "a little dull," as if she'd had one too many drinks. It was so subtle that she didn't realize she wasn't up to par until she started to recover. The lesson she took from these injuries was to pay as much attention to the needs of her own body as to those of her beloved horses. They required regular exercise to keep in shape, and so did she.

Once in the late 1980s she found herself in North Carolina. Everyone was water-skiing. She'd never water-skied before, but it looked like fun and how hard could it be? She was an Olympic athlete after all, and here were all these non-athletes doing the slalom on one ski. It took Anne a good two hours and many attempts before she could get up on one ski! Water-skiing and horseback riding use different muscles and require different skills. Being able to do one sport in high-level competition is no guarantee that you'll be able to do the other without plenty of practice.

In the early 1990s, after she injured her knee, a surgeon told her she needed to be better balanced. When you pursue one sport exclusively, you overuse some muscles and underuse others. "I needed to do exercises to strengthen my legs, my quads, just like the horses' stifles," she says. "You trot them more, gymnasticize them more to protect the joints. And you do your basic dressage and lateral exercises to build the muscles properly in order to keep the horse more sound. The same with us, to be more balanced, you have to cross-train. If it's good enough for Eros, it's good enough for me." She started going to the gym regularly before working out became a nationwide craze. Now there's a gym at Market Street Farm.

Anne's whole life has been devoted to horses and horsemanship. She's not a party person, and she almost never takes vacations, though sometimes she thinks her life would be more balanced if she did. But her life suits her fine; she loves being at home with the horses. For the winter months, she and Hoffy transport a group of horses to Wellington, the famous fairground in Florida, where they have another house. There they continue

Anne With Eros

to train and compete throughout the year. But their life is just as busy in Florida as it is in New Jersey.

Anne is Not Just an Olympic Competitor

Anne still collaborates with Morris today, as she recently did at a 6-day clinic, called the George Morris Horsemastership Training Session in Wellington, Florida, in January of 2009. Top level equestrians gather here to be coached by five different Olympic riders. Anne described her philosophy to journalist Sandy Oliynyk; "It's important to understand fundamental flatwork, how to change your horse's muscles, not through draw reins and big bits, but by using your position to influence your horse ... if you can't control your own body, good luck being able to feel his body and influence [him]."

As if teaching, training, and competing weren't enough, she feels another book germinating inside her. Someday, she wants to write in a way that gives the horse a voice — to use her decades of experience to show people what they can learn from their horses. It's not only the horses that benefit from better horse-to-human communication. The humans can learn a lot too. When you listen to the horse, Anne says, "The horse is trying to tell you that you need to be more aggressive, you need to be more relaxed, or you need to go to the gym, you need to see a sports psychologist ... This is what the horse is trying to tell you." By advocating for the horse's point of view, she hopes she can encourage more people to put themselves in their horses' shoes.

Hopes for the Future

What else does the future hold? Despite her long career in the horse business, Anne isn't jaded. She's still a little amazed that her childhood dream has come true so spectacularly — that she's competed in four Olympic Games and many other top venues. Once she was among the youngest international competitors; now, at forty-nine, she's one of the oldest, and she's still at the top. In some sports, like gymnastics, an athlete is "washed up at eighteen or twenty," but top riders can compete into their fifties. Younger competitors tell her how much they value her wisdom and experience. "Isn't it great to be able to continue to do this?" she asks.

Anne still gets excited about the prospect of a new horse to compete, of seeing how far the horse can go, of training for a possible win at the highest levels, while continuing to be responsive to what the horse needs. She has two that she's competing with now: Champ and Roxana. Roxana's "got the athletic ability, the courage, and the attitude to excel. "She loves it," Anne says. "She attacks the course, saying, 'Thank you for giving me a chance.'" Roxana was short-listed for the U.S. team for the 2008 Hong Kong Olympics and was fourth in the Grand Prix in La Baule in France earlier in the season.

Champ is a lovely nine-year-old Holsteiner stallion; he too was short-listed for the 2008 Olympics. Champ had done so well at Aachen just months before that she felt he was ready, even though she'd only had him for six months. At age nine, he has a big future, so she expects to compete with him at other major venues.

Anne didn't quite make the 2008 U.S. Olympic team; she was the reserve rider, and since the four team members and their horses all stayed sound and healthy, she had to "sit on the bench" in Hong Kong. That was challenging for her, but she says that the thrill of going to the Olympic games is still unsurpassable. "Just being there, having people notice and ask about Champ probably tripled his value," and not long before she had had exhilarating success in the Grand Prix at Aachen and La Baule. Once upon a time she might have worried that she was no longer "good enough," but now she can thoroughly enjoy being with exceptional horses and riders, to have fun being part of the experience of the Olympic Games.

When she comes home to Market Street Farm after many months competing all over the world, "I'm the queen mare in the barn," she says with pleasure. It gives her a good feeling to know that she's paying the bills by doing something that she's passionate about. Turning fifty in 2009, Anne still is healthy and strong and expects to continue doing what she's doing for years to come. Anne says of her horses: "I'm so thankful for all the journeys horses have taken me on. Winning or losing."

Jane Savoie

Dressage Competitor, Olympic Coach & Inspiring Teacher

With Konetta At Wellington, Florida Competition

You better hope that you have obstacles and problems and setbacks, because the only person I know that doesn't have problems is the one in the grave. What I love about an obstacle is it gives me a chance to be creative, to use that right side of my brain to say, 'Okay, what idea or what plan can I come up with that will serve me better?'

Jane Savoie has won nine Horse of the Year awards and three National Freestyle Championships. She competed successfully at the highest levels of international competition and was Reserve Rider for the 1992 Olympic dressage team in Barcelona. She coached U.S. dressage and three-day event riders for the 1996, 2000, and 2004 Olympic Games. Her five acclaimed books include *That Winning Feeling*, which has been translated into several languages and is used by athletes in many sports to improve their performance by overcoming mental roadblocks. She started Dressage Mentor, the first interactive coaching website, in an effort to reach as many riders as possible, without having to travel internationally to give clinics. Riders around the world swear by her instructional videos, and she's much sought after as a lecturer and clinician, while continuing to train and compete with her Friesian, Menno.

Jane On Her Friesian Menno

Despite all this success, she says that she had no business riding for the U. S. Equestrian Dressage Team, nor publishing books, nor lecturing to huge audiences. She did not have the talent. She couldn't afford a world-class horse. She didn't grow up in an equestrian family. She says she got to where she is by "iron-jawed determination." More likely it's because she has made the most of what she was given — and never stopped looking for ways to improve her performance and to help others improve theirs.

Jane described her journey to me as we chatted at the Three Stallion Inn in Randolph, Vermont, not far from Jane's home. It was in June 2005, when rain and fog were just clearing away, exposing the verdant fields and wooded vistas that Jane loves.

Memories of Childhood

Jane grew up in a middle-class home in suburban Boston, the younger of two sisters. As a child, she was hungry for learning. As a kindergartner she remembers coming home crying because she wanted to learn to read. To this day, she listens to instructional tapes while traveling, lest she waste any time. One of her uncles showed her how to develop her memory; when she took tests in high school, she could practically see the relevant page of the textbook in her mind. In the years since, she has been able to acquire and retain new information with little effort.

Her father, Ben Elkind, was "an almost brilliant man" who did not finish high school because he had to help his family during the Depression. He was musical, too; he knew five different instruments and played in bands in his youth. He encouraged Jane to believe she could do whatever she wanted to do in life. Her dad was her first mentor and good friend. As a child, she loved to accompany him on his deliveries for the dry-cleaning business that her grandfather had started. She gravitated to him when he was home from work. The two of them would sit at the kitchen table carding sweaters after they were cleaned and talking for hours. Not a day goes by that Jane doesn't think of her father and wish she could share her life with him.

Ben died of a heart attack at age fifty-three, leaving little money or life insurance. Jane was just eighteen. Weeks before, her parents had deposited her at the University of Massachusetts in Amherst for the start of her freshman year. In the aftermath of her father's death, Jane took over closing the family business, delivering clothing and tying up loose ends, because there was no one else to do it. This was her way. She took charge.

Despite her new responsibilities, she was determined to stay in college. "There was no money when my father died," she says, "so I marched myself right up to the provost's office. I was a freshman there, just a few weeks into school. I said, 'If you want me to stay at your institution, you're going to have to give me a full scholarship because I don't have any money.' I don't know why I thought they'd want me." They did want her and she got a full scholarship!

Her mother, widowed at age forty-six — ten years younger than Jane when we met — went to work as a receptionist, although she had no prior work experience. She supported the family until she remarried a man with whom Jane had an amicable relationship until his recent death. Jane talked to her mother regularly until she passed away in 2009, but always felt a twinge of sadness that her mother didn't seem to get her obsession with horses or the impact she has had on the equestrian world.

Although the family's means were modest, Jane's parents gave her every opportunity to learn new things such as art, swimming, and piano. As a young child, she was "insane" for both dogs and horses. Knowing full well that her parents did not want to take care of a dog, she brought a puppy home and introduced him to her family while peeking through the balusters of the stairway. How could any parents resist? Jane named the puppy Candy. "And of course," she says, "Candy had to be my surrogate horse. I would set up jump courses in the backyard. We'd have lawn chairs with either a broom or a rake across them and he would have to jump the course. I was running beside him, but I went outside the jumps. He was great. He jumped all around the course, and did a little finishing circle and then I used to lunge him. I could put him on a long lead with a whip and he would walk, trot, and canter around me on command."

Jane's flair for performing also blossomed early. She remembers memorizing every song from *Damn Yankees*, which she listened to on the record player and making up dance steps to go with the songs. At five years old she was putting on plays for relatives, complete with commercial announcement breaks.

At a school fair, she won a prize in a coin-toss game: three-inch-high plastic statues of pink and blue horses. They became her stable; the blue ones were geldings and the pink ones were mares.

When Jane was eight, she and her sister got to take horseback riding lessons. Jane was hooked from the start. "My first experience with horses involved all of my senses," she says, looking back. "I'd seen these amazing creatures and I loved all their smells. And hearing the rhythm of the horses trotting along and being able to touch them ... It was total immersion."

From then on, Jane rode at Cherry Ocha Stables in Framingham, Massachusetts. Like many another horse-crazy girl, she worked long hours, mucking out stalls to pay for riding lessons and loving every minute of it. She was a "barn rat," staying there from morning until night in summer and weekends. She rode hunters at Cherry Ocha and loved to jump.

Her first real riding teacher at the barn was a Swedish woman named Inger Svalling, who preferred to be called Marianne. Marianne tracked her down forty-five years later and showed her a video she still had of Jane and her friends "riding the horses bareback, falling off in the snow," Jane remembers. "I really learned how to play with the horses, which is something I got from Marianne. We were at the edge of a reservoir so we swam with the horses. We used to stand up in the saddle, walk, trot and canter and see who fell off first. We would do things like sit sideways on a saddle and do backwards somersaults off the horse while he was moving. We would run up behind the horse and, hands on rump, mount from behind. We did all these crazy tricks, but I think now, never as an adult would I do these things."

When Jane was fourteen, Cherry Ocha Stables was sold. That's how she got Tiny Trooper, a Welsh pony that nobody else wanted. Says Jane: "He was a very difficult horse because he had been originally broken out West and the middle of his tongue was only about one-half inch across because they had put a baling wire around his tongue to break him. So you put any pressure on this horse's mouth, and he would rear. They practically gave him away when they dissolved the place."

When she mounted this horse, Jane remembers, "the second my butt hit the saddle, he just reared straight up." Instinctively Jane knew what to do; she drove the pony forward. If the horse is going forward, it cannot rear. At the merest suggestion of a rear, she would use one rein to put him on a circle and kick until he went forward. Then she would kick him straight out of the circle. After only three weeks of persistent training she had cured Tiny Trooper of rearing.

That pony taught Jane as much as she taught him. "I could never touch his mouth," she says, "but that was another really good thing, because he taught me how to have good soft hands. You couldn't compete with loopy [loose] reins. You had to look like you had contact with your horse's mouth. So I had contact with his mouth, there was no loop, but my hands were that light that he never felt any pressure on his mouth. So he really taught me about having good hands."

Learned to Learn in College – And Met Her Husband Rhett

Once she started college, Jane had less time to ride than she had had as a youngster, but it was there that she was introduced to eventing, in which horse and rider compete in stadium jumping, cross-country, and dressage. It was not love at first sight for Jane and dressage. She loved jumping, but her immediate reaction to dressage was "Boring!" It didn't stay that way.

Her trainer Linda Jaskiel-Brown introduced Jane to dressage as part of the University of Massachusetts combined training program. She participated in Intercollegiate Horse shows and Combined Training events (dressage, stadium jumping, and cross-country) through Preliminary Level. Linda was the first person who made her feel that she had something special to offer as a rider. Inspired by Linda, she reluctantly left the comfortable nest she created at school when she graduated and left the area to resettle in Vermont with her husband.

Jane's college major was animal science; she hoped to go on to veterinary school. In the early 1970s, however, when Jane was applying to vet schools, she discovered that women were not welcome. She was told there was a quota system and a woman's grades and references had to be higher than a man's in order to be accepted. Her adviser discouraged her from applying, but she thinks now that she could have gotten in, because she had high grades and would have had good references.

Looking back, though, she says, "In a way, I'm really happy that I didn't do it because I've been able to do so many other things in my career. Had I been a veterinarian, those avenues would not have been left open to me. I think what I learned how to do in school, which has so enormously helped me in every facet of my career, is that I learned how to study. It wouldn't have mattered if I'd been a business major or an animal science major or a philosophy major. I learned how to organize things" — an invaluable skill for someone who has gone on to write well-organized books and articles about riding and competing.

College changed her life in another momentous way; that was where she met Rhett Savoie, her husband of thirty-five years. The two both complement and inspire each other. Rhett, says Jane, is "very quiet, soft-spoken, not the life of the party type, but he would be the first one to come to the party and the last one to leave because he enjoys people so much. He enjoys listening and taking it in and being a part of it that way. It's a good balance because I'm very erratic. I operate fast-forward. I'm always going at fast speed. I'm mobile and he's very steady. He doesn't get too excited about anything. It's great for me to have Rhett, just by nature of his character, his personality."

In the intervening years, he's also acquired a good eye for telling Jane what she looks like on a horse. On horseback a rider cannot always tell if her body is straight, if her horse's body is straight, or if she is holding tension in her body that is being transmitted to the horse. Rhett plays that role for Jane when she's not with a coach. He's her eyes on the ground.

Dressage as Basis of a Trained, Willing Horse

From love of jumping to dressage – How did Jane make that transition? In the early years of their marriage, money was tight as the Savoies tried to make a living in Vermont, where Rhett's family lived. The first horse Jane could afford to buy was a "broken-down ex-racehorse" named Happenstance, who had a bowed tendon. His $500 purchase price exhausted her life savings — and he couldn't even jump! So she entered wholeheartedly into the world of dressage. In her early twenties, being a goal-oriented person, she set her sights as high as a horsewoman could go, a goal from which she never wavered: to make the United States Equestrian Team in dressage and go to the Olympics.

Dressage, the French word for "training," lays the groundwork for all disciplines of riding. It fosters a partnership between horse and rider that can make any horse more obedient and responsive, flexible and balanced, stronger, more athletic, and more pleasurable to ride. Dressage training enhances the natural movements of the horse. The training gives the horse the ability to use its power more effectively. In its highest forms, horse and rider appear to be performing an elegant duet; imperceptible movements of the rider's seat, legs, and hands elicit apparently effortless responses from the horse.

The regulation-size dressage arena measures 60 by 20 meters with twelve lettered markers on its perimeter. In a dressage test horses must begin and end each movement at the designated letter. The tests are designed to demonstrate the skills of horse and rider in a logical progression, from early training to the highest levels.

In her article "9 Educational Opportunities for the Financially Challenged," Jane recommends that aspiring dressage riders who don't have money for regular lessons or access to excellent trainers use the test descriptions as maps for training themselves. Each level, from Training to Grand Prix, has a stated purpose: for example, at Training Level the purpose is to "confirm that the horse has developed thrust (pushing power) and achieved a degree of balance and throughness." The concept of "throughness" refers to the soft and supple connection that allows the energy of the horse to travel from its hindquarters to the bit. The rider's goal is to preserve the "looseness and suppleness in the muscles and the regularity of the rhythm as the horse covers ground freely forward."

The tests also provide "directive ideas," such as "pay attention to the "quality of the canter, roundness of the circle" for practicing 20-meter circles at the canter. Or for the canter transition, the directive is to achieve a "calmness and smoothness of the depart," a challenge that can take a horse and rider many hours of practice to perform correctly.

The training scale, created by the U.S. Equestrian Federation and the one that the U.S. Dressage Federation (USDF) uses in its tests, includes six ingredients, on which judges evaluate and grade the competitor: Rhythm/Tempo, Suppleness, Contact/Connection, Impulsion, Straightness, and Collection. In the early tests, only the first three are judged. These directives also provide a guide for self-learners, who can practice until their horses have a steady rhythm all around the arena or circle.

Depending on the rider's and horse's level of training, the horse is asked to do extended and collected paces at walk, trot, and canter, to change leads at regular and ever-more-frequent intervals, to perform canter and walk pirouettes, and do such lateral movements as leg-yields, shoulder in, and half-passes. Horse and rider are judged on quality of the paces, impulsion, responsiveness to the rider's subtle aids, and the rider's effectiveness in performing the required test movements. Each movement is judged separately on a scale of 1 to 10, with 10 being the highest.

In the United States, riders compete at Training Level, followed by Levels 1 through 4. The levels recognized by the Fédération Equestre Internationale (FEI) begin with Prix St. Georges, proceed to Intermediare I and II, and culminate in Grand Prix, which is what one sees in international competition. In the *haute école*, the highest level of training taught at the Spanish Riding School and a few other distinguished training sites, horses also do piaffes, or trotting in place, as well as so-called "airs above the ground," such as the spectacular levade, courbette, and capriole. Like reining in the Western tradition, dressage as a competitive sport requires the utmost in precision. It takes immense discipline from the rider to patiently assist the horse to execute the complex maneuvers. But its benefits for training any horse and rider are well documented. Jane Savoie is one of the most avid proponents of dressage in the United States.

Jane Makes the USET "Long List"

Twenty years after Jane set her goal of going to the Olympics, she made the "long list" for the Olympic team — meaning that she was one of twelve dressage riders in the country chosen after a long training and selection process. She made it to Reserve rider at the Barcelona Olympics in 1992 on Zapatero, a horse purchased for her in 1989 by a company for the intention of competing in the Olympics. In Jane's words, Zapatero was "an amazing horse ... small, but moved like a big horse. He tried his heart out." By this time she was 42. But, much training and competing had to go on before she was "long listed" for the Olympics.

Once Jane set her goal of getting to the Olympics when she was only in her twenties, she studied with some exemplary trainers. Cindy Sydnor was one of the first; Cindy has been a distinguished dressage coach and judge with the U.S. Equestrian Federation and an examiner for the USDF instructor certification program. She studied with one of the senior riders from the Spanish Riding School of Vienna.

Jane and Rhett had recently moved to Vermont at the time she began to work with Cindy and she was working as a waitress. She was able to save enough tip change to take a couple of two-day clinics each year. She didn't even own a truck or trailer, she had to borrow from friends and haul Happenstance to Hamilton, Massachusetts, where Cindy was training. But she loved the lessons and soaked up every bit of information and took it back home to practice, practice, practice.

Eventually, she made more money giving lessons at a nearby barn and was able to train with six-time Olympian Robert Dover, who has remained a friend and coach, as well as with other luminaries in Europe. She became interested in sports psychology, read everything she could get her hands on, and as a speed reader from her early school years, she was able to absorb what she read and apply it to training herself and her students. She was an avid fan of Alois Podhajsky, former director of the Spanish Riding School and himself an Olympic dressage competitor; his book *The Complete Training of Horse and Rider* became her bible. Her routine was to read a section of the book, then get on her horse to practice what she'd just read.

There were many other books that were her constant companions as she trained herself, with little money available for high-level coaches, to excel enough to consider competing at the upper levels. Some of the books she has loved were Sally Swift's *Centered Riding; Practical Dressage* by Jane Kidd; *Feel the Fear and Do It Anyway* by Susan Jeffers; and anything by Anthony Robbins. Jane has always been a voracious reader and learner. This quality made it possible for her to train herself to meet her goal, despite the fact that she had little money.

The long road to the U.S.Olympic team, the most prestigious and demanding of the USET competitions, begins when a qualified rider files her intention to compete. Next comes a series of selection trials, at each of which she is scored and ranked. Jane made the long list of 12 and then, after further trials, she was named to the short list for the Olympic squad – of all the competitors in dressage in the country, she made the short list of six competitors! But, when competing in Europe in one of the last trials, she rode one good test and one not so good. She didn't make the starting squad, but she did become the Reserve rider, the one who would fill in if one of the starters couldn't compete. What got in her way?

Her "raging insecurity" emerged full-force, she says; she kept telling herself that she wasn't "in the same league with the other equestrians on that list, no way." She was also smoking three packs of cigarettes a day and was twenty-five pounds heavier than she is now! If she really wanted to ride for the United States in the Olympics, she would have to drastically change her lifestyle.

She resolved to tackle her insecurities head-on. In about 1987, she discovered Maxwell Maltz's *Psychocybernetics*. The book changed her life. Maltz suggested that relying on "iron-jawed determination" — accessing only conscious thoughts and attitudes, a method that Jane thought had served her well in the past — would lead to only temporary changes. But "in a much gentler, simpler way," Jane explains, "if you direct your effort toward the part of your brain that truly controls your actions, your subconscious mind, you can make long-lasting, permanent changes. I learned how to program my subconscious mind so that I could get what I wanted."

Maltz described how to communicate with the subconscious through visualization. Jane applied this to riding and competing on horseback. "Whenever I wanted to practice the entry to a dressage test or competition," she says, "I would, in my mind's eye, be riding that test, stride for stride for stride. I would be seeing the perfect picture in great detail, adding things like hearing the rhythm of the horse's footfall, feeling the weight of the reins, smelling the fly spray, tasting the salty perspiration dripping down underneath my hard hat. I'd get all my five senses involved, so the visualization was vivid. And then I'd involve emotion. I'd feel a sense of calmness and poise when I was outside the arena. I would have this feeling of gratitude wash over me. To do a good visualization, it's a combination of your creative right brain, your logical left brain, and your emotional midbrain, and done on a spaced repetition."

Another of Maltz's methods that Jane took to heart and applied to her equestrian career is positive self-talk. To achieve a goal, you address yourself as if you've already achieved it: "I am a relaxed competitor," not "I will be a relaxed competitor." And you focus on the positives, not the negatives. If you tell yourself, "I am not nervous," your unconscious mind screens out the "not" and hears "I am nervous." So instead you tell yourself, "I am calm."

At the highest levels of competition, Jane explains, competitors are equally skilled, their horses all impeccably prepared. What distinguishes one from another is "what is going on between your ears," she says. This is where discipline and control come into play. To achieve consistent success, a rider must be able to manage any fears, negativity, or insecurities time after time, despite the weather, lack of sleep, the horse's mood, or deep-seated conviction that a rival can't be defeated.

Her long time coach Robert Dover is another advocate of visualization and positive self-talk. He likes to say, "You act like a champion before you are a champion."

Robert Dover played a key role in the selection trials for the Barcelona Olympics. Jane was riding Zapatero. "We were warming up and time was running out, and we have to be in the arena on time or you're eliminated," Jane recalls. "And we have to do flying lead changes every other stride for the Grand Prix test. Could not get the flying changes every other stride to save my life. Time was running out. And Robert says, 'Okay, you're on, off you go!' And I looked at him and said, 'What about the two tempis?' And he said, 'They're going to be perfect!' And that's exactly the way he thinks. So I went to the test, and his words just rang through my brain and I said, 'They're going to be perfect.' And they were. Clocked them off like there never had been any problem."

Coach to Olympic Teams and Beloved Teacher

While going through the paces to qualify for the selection trials in Atlanta in 1996, Jane planned to try out on a horse called Eastwood, but the horse became very ill and had to have a kidney removed. So she was suddenly out of the running for the Olympics.

Serendipitously, Peter Gray, the coach of the Canadian Three-Day Event team in Atlanta, who knew her because she had trained individuals like Kelli Temple and Stuart Black, Canadian long-list competitors, asked her to coach the team on the dressage part of the three-day event. This established her as a coach for Olympic-aspiring teams and launched the career that has fulfilled her for many years. Later she was asked to coach individual riders in Sydney in 2000 and coach Jimmy Wofford asked her to coach competitors in Athens in 2004. She began to realize that she loved to teach and coach, that she had a gift as a teacher. She struggled with this for years, haunted by that decades-long dream of representing the United States on the Olympic dressage team. A teacher? She always dreamed of being a competitor, a great rider!

It took a few more years, but eventually she got it: "The purpose of my life is to be an inspired and inspiring teacher. I fought that, tooth and nail, for a while, but that was my gift. I wanted my gift to be that I was a brilliant rider, but, sorry, that's not my gift. My gift is not in my riding. I'm a good rider. I'm an adequate rider. I'm a gifted teacher."

Her friend Jane Ashley described her: "What you do is so much more than teaching riding. It's so much more than teaching people the mechanics of a shoulder in or a leg yield. You teach people how to set goals. You teach people how to believe in themselves. You teach people how to organize their thinking. What you're doing goes so far beyond teaching horseback riding."

Balance and Self Healing

Jane has taken her teaching and coaching talents in myriad directions. She began producing training videotapes and became a sought-after speaker at a wide variety of sports psychology, motivational, and equestrian conferences. Between riding, competing, coaching, running clinics, writing books and journal articles, and trying her hand at creating DVDs, she was, and still is, someone who has a hard time relaxing.

Some years ago, she realized she was burning out. She went to see a chiropractor who told her she had to get more balance in her life. She could not work seven days a week. This was a hard habit to change for a high-energy person who needed continuous action and movement, both physically and mentally. She vowed to take some time off and restore herself.

How do you do that? Jane discovered fishing, of all things. It was totally unrelated to the horse business, and it offered a way to be alone and sit still. Later, she learned to relax by going to movies in the afternoon, all by herself. Just Jane and her bag of popcorn. This she continues to do every couple of weeks. It's a perfect way of winding down, laughing, and discharging energy from her usually frenetic life. It's a way of maintaining her emotional balance.

Although it is horse-related and takes deep concentration, she also gets a feeling of balance while she is writing. "So much of what I do between teaching and lecturing at the expos and symposiums and workshops is oriented to the public. I like the writing because it's solitary and quiet, so I find a balance that way as well. To be able to go off by myself in this little cocoon of concentration and there's nobody else out there and I don't have to interact with other people."

Jane notes that this is what we do when we ride a horse, we find our balance. She tries to do this in her life as well. Ruth Poulsen, the woman who runs her barn now, is another such calming influence in her life. So is her mother-in-law. To be a professional equestrienne at a high level takes immense concentration and focus. It is all-consuming. But Jane recognizes that balance is important for her, so she consciously makes space for other things in her life.

One way she has expanded her consciousness in recent years is to learn about healing arts. Like all riders, she has had injuries that caused pain. When she was thirty, a stallion got loose and kicked her with both hind feet. It nearly killed her. She had all her front teeth kicked out and her upper jaw broken. For years she could chew only in the back of her mouth, which was constantly throbbing. The chronic pain wore her down. This accident put a fear in her. To this day, she is wary as she walks behind any horse.

As a teacher and coach, she has come across many students who have fears, some realistic and based on their own mishaps with horses and others that stem from other sources. Jane loves finding new healing techniques to help her students, friends, and family recover from fears and from physical and mental discomfort, just as she has found ways to heal herself.

One of these healing arts is called Emotional Freedom Technique, which employs tapping on the endpoints of acupuncture meridians. Since our systems are composed of energy, according to EFT, a negative emotion or sensation is caused by a disruption in the energy system. Developed by Gary Craig, it is simply a way of rebalancing negative energy in our systems, Jane explains. She has used it for all types of problems, including menstrual cramps, phobias about going over bridges, or fears about the next dressage test. It's a way she can both help others and teach people how to help themselves. Helping to heal others is one of the things "that keeps me passionate about what I do. It's still under the umbrella of horses, but I feel like I'm going off in so many different directions. I'm learning things at such an incredible rate that I can hardly keep up with myself."

Jane's successful first book, *That Winning Feeling*, has had many printings and has been translated into six languages. The most autobiographical of her writings, it is based on her search to find ways to overcome the insecurities that have held her back. She realizes that "the inside of you is always looking at the outside of everybody else. So the inside of you feels inadequate, insecure, anxious and looks at the outside of people like Linda Tellington-Jones and thinks, I wish I had my act together like she does. But then you realize that the inside of her is probably looking at the outside of everyone else and thinking the same thing." (See Linda's story.)

Jane did what came naturally to her. She researched methods to heal herself and to enhance her performances. She discovered the concepts of visualization and positive self-talk. She gives an example of how she uses visualization.

"My horse's left hind leg is his weaker one. And even in warm-up today, going through the corners rather than doing a single thing with my aids, I visualized his left hind leg being placed where I wanted it to be, underneath his body, rather than unloading it and placing it to the inside. I use visualization with the horses because I believe there's some sort of connection between what you're thinking and what's going on with your horse and you can communicate psychically like that."

Jane points out that studies have been done with athletes where they

Jane On Moshi

have measured the firing of the muscles with an electromyogram and have discovered that the muscles do the exact same thing whether the athlete is visualizing or physically performing the exercise. "If you picture in your mind's eye vividly the perfect shoulder-in, the perfect leg yield, the perfect canter transition, your muscles are going to fire in such a way to create that picture that you have in your mind's eye."

She has used those methods to achieve goals small and large, ever since. When she and Rhett first moved to central Vermont, she was waitressing and wished she could be teaching riding. She visualized her appointment book completely scheduled up and said to herself repeatedly, "I'm the most sought-after instructor in Vermont." Before long, she was the most sought-after instructor in Vermont. She did the same thing, after seeing a gorgeous Friesian horse at Equitana, the big horse exposition. She decided she must have a Friesian and visualized it in minute and concrete detail. Within two years, her dream came true, when Proud Meadow Farm in Texas bought her the wonderful Friesian called Menno that she rides and competes now.

Jane's Valued Role Models and Teachers

Another important influence in Jane's equestrian life has been Pam Goodrich, who taught her to be more right-brained. "I am very left-brained. I'm a list maker, I make outlines. When I teach, my friends call what I do 'recipe riding.' If you add a pinch of this and a dash of that and you stir it all together, then you get a horse that's doing such and such."

Jane's cross-training books reflect that left-brain way of thinking. She made a list of every possible combination of aids and what they communicate to the horse. She included what each seat bone, leg, and rein action would say so that the horse does not have to "play multiple-choice." That is her strength, and it has served her well in many circumstances. It has also limited her in some ways, she sees now. *A Happy Horse*, which consists of 23 progressive lessons on CD and DVD, with an accompanying workbook, is designed to meet all learner's styles. It reflects Jane's capacity to break down any movement into its smallest parts, so that the rider-student and horse know exactly what to do. It teaches using her left-brain strengths, but Jane came to understand these movements more effectively by being able to visualize, a right-brain strength.

Pam Goodrich helped her to use right-brain functioning; now she sees her right brain as being as adept as her left. Although it was a struggle for her to activate that part of her brain, Pam, who is a gifted teacher and rider, spurred her on to loosen up her capacity for imagery and sensation, rather than relying on logic and rationality only. Training with Pam helped her to get a picture in her mind of the balance and carriage she wanted her horse to have.

Two other equestriennes who have influenced Jane are Sue Blinks and Cindy Sydnor. Sue's commitment to the welfare of the horse is paramount. Recognizing this was crucial for Jane, who, being a conscientious student, had wanted to please her instructor at all costs. This sometimes got in the way of being a true advocate for her horse. You are the one who can best judge if your mount needs to rest, regardless of your instructor's advice from the ground. Sue's modeling of being an advocate for her horse has made an impact on Jane; never does she subordinate her horse's needs to her own desires.

Cindy Sydnor has the same dedication to the welfare of the horse. She also believes that "you ask often, expect little, and reward generously." Jane has adapted that philosophy to teaching students as well as training horses.

A gifted teacher who has gleaned experience and information from a variety of sources, Jane, who once thought dressage was "boring," finds it now "endlessly interesting." She imagines herself as a physical therapist of the horse, who examines the horse's movements to determine where he is locked, blocked, weak, or sore. Then she prescribes a way to unlock, unblock, strengthen or soothe the horse so that he can perform at his best. She learned from Cindy Sydnor how to organize a lesson and determine your horse's physical therapy needs and how to communicate that to the rider.

Jane's unstoppable passion for learning, challenging herself, and competing brought her to yet another epiphany. She has availed herself of trainings with Tony Robbins, the celebrated motivational coach. In her motivational books she talks about neuro-associative conditioning, a concept she got from Robbins, whose book, *Awaken the Giant Within,* inspired her even before she trained with him. Jane describes the serendipitous circumstances in which she decided to take his course after ordering his new tape series.

"There's a coupon in it for $100 off for one of his live seminars and

I'm in West Palm Beach [her winter training ground] and he's going to be in Orlando, which is three hours away. I thought, 'Oh my God, when am I ever going to be that physically close that I can drive to see Tony Robbins?' So I call up the Tony Robbins Company and I said, 'What does it cost with this $100 off.' They told me it costs $989. I got off the phone and I call up the credit card company and a little mechanical electrical voice comes on, and says, 'You have $989 of available credit.' It wasn't $988, it wasn't $990. It was to the dollar what I needed."

This was the first of several Tony Robbins' seminars she attended. In one of them, three thousand people did a fire-walk on a bed of eighteen-hundred-degree coals with not one getting burned feet. Robbins demonstrates how to get into a mental state where you do not get burned. Jane has since done four of Robbins' programs, including one in Fiji with her husband, where they had to climb a sixty-five-foot-high swaying pole and then, when you get to the top, you have to let go and jump into thin air to grab a trapeze. These experiments have excited and challenged Jane. They keep her always in a state of becoming. She never seems to stand still.

Giving Back

Jane likes the feeling of helping others and making an impact on their lives. She knows she has had incredible opportunities because of others' generosity and she wants to give back to people in the way she has received. Her notoriety gives her a sense of the responsibility she has as a public person. She gets many letters; in one that particularly affected her, the writer wrote "that she had a brain tumor and that she was going through chemotherapy. The writer said, 'I just want you to know that every time my husband takes me in for my chemo treatment, I bring two things with me — I bring your book, and I bring the little picture that you sent me. And this is how I get through my chemo sessions. You are the angel on my shoulder.'"

Another way that Jane found to give back to the community occurred after September 11, 2001. She had been out of the country on the day the towers were toppled, but when she returned she discovered that her stepfather's daughter had been on one of the planes. She was immobilized by the tragedy and it was even more painful to find that someone she knew had been a victim. In despair for a while, she decided to take action.

Celebrities were on television raising big money for victims, and she tried to imagine what she could do with her own set of skills to match the work those luminaries were doing. She hit upon an idea, one that gave her much satisfaction. In three weeks she made arrangements to offer a benefit training at the beautiful equine facility of the late Charles Bronson.

"We had red, white, and blue bunting all over the place," she remembers, "patriotic music, red, white, and blue doughnuts. I called up every tack store in the area to ask them to make a donation for a silent auction. It was $30 per person, so that no one felt it was above their means and that if they wanted to put a little more money in the pot, that was fine. I did this seminar with demo horses. And at $30 a head we made $8,300 for the United Way fund that afternoon. And it felt great, as you could imagine. It felt fabulous."

She also used her contacts with *Dressage Today* and other equine magazines in the Primedia group and got them to place notices in their next issue, urging equestrians all around the country to do the same kind of benefit for 9/11 victims. She was gratified that there was such a tremendous response. It was a turning point in her life to do what Tony Robbins calls changing her "primary question." In the past, she saw herself as being self-absorbed. Her primary question involved how she was feeling, how she was doing. Now she changed that question to "What can I do to help others?" And it feels so much more satisfying to her to help others and to have the stature to be able to do that.

Tony Robbins taught about six basic human needs – for variety, consistency, connection to others, sense of significance, growth, and contribution. You can live with only the first four, he says, but if you also have the last two – growth and contribution, then you are a fulfilled individual. Jane recognizes the value of contribution now. No longer is she reliant on merely feeling significant. She wants to contribute to others' well-being, not just her own.

What lies ahead for this multi-talented woman? She has competed at high levels, coached Olympic-level competitors, trained horses and riders, given motivational talks, written books, made training videos, and done radio shows.

A few years ago, Jane thought her next challenge would be to produce television programs pertaining to the equestrian world. She started studying others who have done so, people who happen to be Western riders. She recognizes that you can learn from everybody, even if they are not from your discipline, as long as you keep your mind open. You build "an eclectic system where you take a little bit from everybody that has something of value." She can learn from Western riders the technical aspects of what makes a TV show exceptional. Whether or not she decides to venture into the TV world, she knows that it is not the destination, but rather the journey that you have to love. You have to be passionate about the day-to-day process of what you are doing, whatever that is. And, for someone who loves learning new things, Jane is always going to be passionate about something.

Epilogue

What Can We Learn From These Winners?

These thirteen women from English and Western equestrian disciplines shared from their hearts what it has been like for them to learn, practice, and excel in sports where women were not always welcomed.

The women were from all over the United States and one, Linda Tellington-Jones, grew up in western Canada. They were ages forty through ninety and all of them were still engaged in equestrian activities when I interviewed them. The late Sally Swift, who was over ninety when I met her, was no longer riding and teaching, but she remained an active ambassador of her training programs and her books, the last of which she published at age 90.

All of the women, regardless of their age, represent an ideal of positive aging. They competed, won, coached, trained, created new programs and methods, published books, and challenged convention into their fifties, sixties, and beyond.

What has been the women's formula for success and fulfillment? Although I didn't ask them this question, their stories yield information about what is common among them. I expected to meet people who came from equestrian families or who had affluent parents capable of funding their daughters' horse passions. At the least, I imagined that all of their parents would have promoted their child's interests in horses. I was surprised to discover that this was not always the case.

All of the women had an early, sometimes passionate attraction to horses or to animals in general. Cutting champion Lindy Burch and dressage competitor Jane Savoie each tried to become a veterinarian. Jane was dissuaded because she was told that women were not accepted in vet school in the 1960s. Lindy applied and failed to gain acceptance, but went on to study and teach biological sciences before she decided that cutting was her first love. Both Lindy and Jane are gratified that they took the route they did. They recognize that their careers have become so much more fruitful than they ever imagined – being able to teach, coach, breed horses, compete, write, and be a public figure who is sought after all over the country, if not internationally.

Several of the women bore losses, such as divorce, illness, and death of loved ones, but stayed the course, despite these setbacks. Race-rider Julie Krone was devastated by her parents' divorce as a child, and then again in early adulthood when her mother, who was her first equestrian teacher and always-booster, died as a young woman from cancer. "I was overflowing with drive and determination and nothing was going to get in the way of my success," said Julie, barely daunted by her difficult history. Former trick rider Karen Vold was similarly affected by her parents' divorce as a youngster, but "I have great perseverance and a no-quit philosophy," she told me proudly.

Barrel racer Sharon Camarillo and visionary healer Linda Tellington-Jones, report poignantly about their abusive marriages, which each ended in divorce after many years of being victimized, both physically and mentally. Linda states that she curiously just remembers the positive, even about the bad times. Sharon felt that she grew more resilient and wouldn't be the strong person she is, had it not been for her tumultuous marriage. They both had a talent for finding the silver lining behind the dark clouds.

Both Sally Swift and Valerie Kanavy endured physical challenges as children. Sally had scoliosis, which affected much of her activity and probably compelled her into using horseback riding as a palliative. Valerie had a serious polio episode as a child and was not expected to survive it with any mobility, let alone by being a world-class endurance champion. Both may have been spurred on by these disabilities to compensate for the vulnerability.

Many of the women were willing to take risks. With some, it was taking a physical risk by pushing themselves past what they presumed to be their limits on a horse. Roberta McCarty, after studying the equestrian books she amassed, tried out whatever she saw pictures of. After seeing movies of the famed Spanish Riding School in Vienna, she figured out a way to get her horse so riled up by racing up and down the arena and stopping suddenly, that he would eventually lift up his front legs in a stunning cabjole.

These women took up challenges, pushed their limits, and exceeded even their own expectations as they climbed the ladder of competitions in all fields. Sure, they had doubts at times. Valerie Kanavy had to be encouraged by her husband to try for a world championship; she had hesitated, thinking she'd been so successful in local endurance races, why push her luck? But he challenged her: ride to win — instead of just to finish, as is the mantra for many endurance riders. And win she did, several times and is still planning to enter more international races at age sixty. Still, she mused, she reminds herself that this is just horse-racing and that the most important thing is for her to be remembered as a good person.

These women never stop learning. Most have an intense curiosity that propels them to want to learn all they can about their sport, about taking the best care of their horses, and about forming a relationship with the horses they encounter. It's another way they challenge themselves. Jane Savoie sums up her philosophy: "You better hope you have obstacles and problems... What I love about an obstacle is it give me a chance to be creative, to use that right side of my brain to say, 'What idea or what plan can I come up with that will serve me better?' "

These "women who could – and did" have provided me endless hours of joy while meeting them in their barns and ranches, in writing their inspirational stories, and in receiving their wisdom, not only about horses, but about life. They have become role models for me of resiliency, determination, passion, and genuineness.

Photo Credits

Linda Tellington-Jones: p. 1 ©Mike Brinson with permission; p. 16 ©Karma Kitaj's personal collection

Valerie Kanavy: p. 17 ©Genie Stewart-Spears with permission; p. 25 ©Genie Stewart-Spears with permission

Lindy Burch: p. 33 ©*NCHA Cutting Horse Chatter*
p. 43 ©Cappy Jackson with permission;
p. 45 ©Sally Harrison with permission

Julie Krone: p. 47 & 55 ©Don Krone with permission; p. 60 ©Karma Kitaj's personal collection

Kathy Kusner: p. 72 ©Karma Kitaj's personal collection

Carol Kozlowski: p. 77 & p.88 ©Hoofpics by Pam Eckelbarger with permission

Roberta McCarty: p. 93 ©Daryl Weisser with permission; p. 104 ©Woltenberry, with permission

Karen Womack Vold: p. 112 ©Karma Kitaj's personal collection; p. 119 ©Photos By Gerry with permission of Gerry Hoff

Sharon Camarillo: p. 125 ©Cyndy Smith; p. 127 ©ProSportsPix with permission

Sally Swift: p. 141, Courtesy of Trafalgar Square Books, @Darrell Dodds, photographer; p. 154, ©Karma Kitaj's personal collection

Lucile Bump: p. 155 ©Karma Kitaj's personal collection

Anne Kursinski: p. 161 ©Janice Syphers, photographer with permission; p. 173 ©Sue Kyllonen

Jane Savoie: p. 177, ©Susan Sexton; p. 178, ©Rhett Savoie with permission; p.191 ©Rhett Savoie with permission

Karma Kitaj Bio Photo: p. 210 ©Barbara Simundza with permission

It is with deep gratitude that we acknowledge these photographers who have donated their photos to this project. Their generosity is greatly appreciated. We have made every attempt to locate the photographers who are responsible for a few very old photos. Any information about them would be appreciated.

Index

About the Author

Karma Kitaj, PhD, has 30+ years of experience as a certified life coach, specializing in the over-50 demographic and retirement lifestyle planning, as a licensed psychotherapist, a published author of *Women Who Could... and Did: Lives of 26 Exemplary Artists and Scientists* (2002), and a motivational speaker who addresses audiences about peak performance and creating new lifestyles after leaving your mid-years' career.

Karma went back to graduate school for a PhD in her 40s after her 101 year old grandmother asked her, a practicing social worker, "When are you going to finish your studies?" She was Visiting Research Scholar in the 1990s at the Stone Center, Wellesley College Centers for Women, where she conducted the research and analysis of the interviews for her first book.

She authors a blog called "Retirement As You Want It" (www.RetirementAsYouWantIt.com) including "Tips, resources, interviews, and reviews for Baby Boomers and beyond who want to embrace new experiences and create meaning in the next step of their lives." Karma writes columns for various ezines, including one on "Meaning and Purpose" for www.WorkForce50.com and for www.Boomerous.com. She hosts a TV series called "ALivelihood: New Careers As We Age" on www.BATV.org.

In her middle-age, Karma became a horse-back riding enthusiast, even though she was never athletic as a kid, avoiding sweating at all costs. She is exhilarated about challenging her body to learn a new sport. She went all over the country to interview women for this book, meeting people in their ranches and barns from New Jersey to Florida to Hawaii.

See Karma's blog, www.RetirementAsYouWantIt.com and websites, www.LifeSpringCoaching.com and www.HuckleHillPress.com. She can be reached for speaking and coaching engagements at 617.731.6170 or at Karma@LifeSpringCoaching.com.

Women Riders Who Could ... And Did — Order Form

Email orders: Use PayPal button at www.LifeSpringCoaching.com or email Info@HuckleHillPress.com with the information below.
Telephone orders: (617) 731 6170; (have credit card ready)

Mail Postal orders: Huckle Hill Press
PO Box 67273
Chestnut Hill, MA 02467

Bill to:

Name ____________________

Organization ____________________

E-mail address (to permit you to track shipping) ____________________

Mailing Address ____________________

City ____________________ State __________ Zip __________

Phone (______) ____________________

❑ *Ship to the above address:*

Ship to a different address: ____________________

Name ____________________

Mailing Address ____________________

City ____________________ State __________ Zip __________

Phone (______) ____________________

Women Riders Who Could...And Did Book $21.95
Women Who Could...And Did: Lives of 26 Exemplary Artists & Scientists Book $16.95
Both books for $29.95

First Class Shipping (within the U.S.) Add $4.95 for one book or call (617) 731-6170 for more than one book

Total $__________

❑ Check enclosed for $__________

❑ Charge my Visa or Master Card credit card $__________ #: ____________________

Three digit ID ____________________ Exp. date ____________________

Call (617) 731-6170 if ordering for shipping costs outside the U.S. Allow 2 weeks for shipping.

Bulk discount available for 5 or more copies sent to the same address. If you represent a company that wants to use this book as a premium gift, please contact publisher for information about discounts.

Ask for personalized autograph and author will be happy to provide it.